THE FEDERAL
ANTITRUST LAWS

THE FEDERAL ANTITRUST LAWS

Third Revised Edition

Jerrold G. Van Cise

American Enterprise Institute for Public Policy Research
Washington, D. C.

Jerrold G. Van Cise is a partner in the law firm of Cahill Gordon and Reindel in New York. He was formerly chairman of the Section on Antitrust Law of the New York State Bar Association and chairman of the Section of Antitrust Law of the American Bar Association. He was also a member of the Attorney General's National Committee to Study the Antitrust Laws.

ISBN 0-8447-3173-0

Domestic Affairs Study 33, August 1975

Second printing, May 1977

Library of Congress Catalog Card No. 75-18568

First Edition 1962. Revised Edition 1965.
Second Revised Edition 1967.

Printed in the United States of America

CONTENTS

1

THE ANTITRUST PARADOX

The businessman tends to view our antitrust laws with restrained enthusiasm. In *principle*, he reluctantly acknowledges that he should favor their provisions; but, as a *principal*, he seldom displays any fondness for their prohibitions. He admits that he must live with this legislation, for better or for worse, yet he finds it difficult to return its embrace with any degree of affection.

Thus, in principle, a businessman usually concedes that he should favor the antitrust laws because history seems to have recorded their necessity. In the past, he knows, the noble experiment of governmental "hands off" of business—or laissez faire—had been attempted both here and abroad. Private restraints of oppressive conspiracies and predatory monopolies had thereupon sprung up in industry after industry—injurious equally to small competitor, to laborer, and to consumer—and these business abuses had over the years forced the return to varying degrees of governmental intervention. For example, in some countries, this failure of laissez faire had caused hostile governments to eliminate these private restraints by the simple expedient of eliminating the existence of private business. Again, in other countries, distrustful governments had acted to correct these private restraints by eliminating the freedom of private business. But in this and some other countries, fortunately, more tolerant governments had dealt with the private restraints by seeking to eliminate only the private restraints themselves, through the antitrust laws. These laws, therefore, are generally acknowledged[1] to be necessary in order to protect industry, on the one hand, from the private restraints of antisocial business action and, on the other, from the alternative

---

[1] See, for example, *Report of the Attorney General's National Committee to Study the Antitrust Laws* (1955), pp. 1–2. Hereinafter cited as *Report*.

public restraints of anti-business socialists. The businessman may dislike the King Log of antitrust prohibitions for interfering with his freedom of action, but he usually dreads far more the King Stork of confiscation.

As a principal, however, the businessman is not fond of the antitrust laws, because they threaten him with substantial fines, years in jail, injunctions, divestiture, and treble damages for violation of statutes which fail to specify, with precision, what he may and may not do. He is painfully aware that the words of these statutes are, for the most part, undefined; that their interpretations by the courts are frequently unreliable; and, accordingly, that the application of these statutes and their interpretations are at times unpredictable. He is further conscious that the restraints sought to be *pro*scribed in one industry may, by regulatory statutes, be *pre*scribed in another. It is difficult, therefore, for a businessman to display more than cold correctness toward any statutory prohibitions whose imposition of criminal and civil sanctions may—in the words of our highest court—represent "inconsistency and illogic of long standing."[2]

This paradox of mental acceptance, but emotional rejection, of our antitrust laws by the business community has suggested the need for a monograph, such as this, written for the lay reader.[3] The necessity for some such laws is assumed. The following analysis of the specific statutes will thereupon concede to the business executive that the provisions of these laws are inconclusive, that their interpretations are inconsistent, and that their application on occasion is uncertain. It will attempt to demonstrate to him, however, why these laws in their day-to-day operation are, and probably must continue to be, such an irrational thorn in his commercial flesh. Like a psychiatrist, this little work will not seek to cure—but rather through better understanding endeavor to help the businessman cope with—this necessarily elusive legislation. For the reader seeking more detailed information, footnotes have been added in order to refer him to illustrative authorities on the subject matter of the text, which he may borrow from his attorney's library.

The temptation also to explore in this monograph the further paradox of the enactment by Congress both of "anti" and "pro" trust laws will be resisted. While the right hand of our federal legislature has prohibited restraints of trade generally in our economy, in the manner outlined in these pages, its left hand, by special exemptions

---

[2] Flood v. Kuhn, 407 U.S. 258, 284 (1972).
[3] For a parallel publication covering more technical details of interest to the practicing lawyer, see Jerrold G. Van Cise, *Understanding the Antitrust Laws* (New York: Practicing Law Institute, 1973).

and regulatory statutes, has permitted such conduct in certain segments of industry and labor. Examples of this latter encouragement of trade restraints are those directed to fair trade, export associations, communication, transportation, and agriculture.[4] Whether our business community can thus continue to be a house divided—part a free economy and part a slave to public and private regimentation—is a controversial story that is best told elsewhere.

It should suffice for our present purposes to state that the courts are deeply troubled by this Janus-faced approach to competition;[5] and—while they may recognize the jurisdiction of a regulatory agency to defer[6] or to defeat[7] the application of the antitrust laws to industrial conduct—they nevertheless require such an agency at least to consider both the regulatory and the antitrust policies in its rulings.[8] The quasi-monopolist of a regulated industry should not lightly assume that his license to engage in that business necessarily authorizes him to deprive others of their economic liberty;[9] and even the privileged labor union must stop, look, and listen before guiding wage negotiations into a collision course with our laws on trade regulation.[10]

Indeed, one who claims to be exempt from the antitrust laws today must assume the burden of proof to establish this immunity,[11] because the courts either will not or "cannot lightly assume that the enactment of a special regulatory scheme for particular aspects of an industry was intended to render the more general provisions of the antitrust laws wholly inapplicable to that industry."[12]

In short, a businessman who is convinced against his will of the desirability of the antitrust laws—and is reluctant to comply with their commands—should hesitate to be of the opinion still that he may join with impunity the many who may yet flout these statutes. It is true that there may be some safety in numbers, but he will find far greater safety in exodus.

---

[4] See, for example, *Report*, pp. 108–14, 149–55, 261, et seq.
[5] See, for example, Pan American World Airways, Inc., v. United States, 371 U.S. 296 (1963).
[6] Ricci v. Chicago Mercantile Exchange, 409 U.S. 289 (1973).
[7] Hughes Tool Co. v. Trans World Airlines, Inc., 409 U.S. 363 (1973).
[8] Gulf States Utilities Company v. Federal Power Commission, 411 U.S. 747 (1973); Port of Portland v. United States, 408 U.S. 811 (1972).
[9] Silver v. New York Stock Exchange, 373 U.S. 341 (1963).
[10] United Mine Workers of America v. Pennington, 381 U.S. 657 (1965); but cf. American Federation of Musicians v. Joseph Carroll, 391 U.S. 99 (1968).
[11] United States v. First City National Bank of Houston, 386 U.S. 361 (1967).
[12] Carnation Company v. Pacific Westbound Conference, 383 U.S. 213, 218 (1966); also Federal Maritime Commission v. Aktiebolaget Svenska Amerika Linien, 390 U.S. 238 (1968).

2

THE PROVISIONS OF THE ANTITRUST LAWS

Legislative Principles

The antitrust laws are most readily approached by the lay reader if he realizes that they embody two fundamental principles, which give an underlying unity to their provisions.

The first basic principle of these laws is that their general objective is to prohibit private restraints that may operate to deny to our nation a competitive economy: "the purpose was . . . to make of ours, so far as Congress could under our dual system, a competitive business economy."[1]

To achieve this objective, therefore, the laws contain sweeping provisions directed against private—as distinguished from governmental[2]—restraints which threaten such a competitive economy. Congress has wisely declined to narrow these prohibitions to a precise condemnation of enumerated restraints, on the ground that to do so would, on the one hand, handicap business by inflexible rigidity and, on the other hand, facilitate evasion of its legislative commands through failure to list all forms of anti-competitive conduct.[3]

Thus it is obvious that any meticulous itemization by Congress of prohibited practices would work to the disadvantage of private industry. This is because specific conduct might reasonably be singled out for legislative proscription in most settings, but it could be in the public interest to permit it in some. For example, condemnation of joint buying and joint selling by competitors might be appropriate for

---

[1] United States v. South-Eastern Underwriters Association, 322 U.S. 533, 599 (1944).
[2] Federal Communications Commission v. RCA Communications, Inc., 346 U.S. 86 (1953).
[3] Appalachian Coals, Inc. v. United States, 288 U.S. 344 (1933).

many industries,[4] but it would be ruinous in the investment banking industry.[5] Again, a definition of illegal monopolization as a person seeking to control 90 percent of the trade might be justified for large[6] producers of basic commodities competing in a national market, but any such determination would be unrealistic for the only theater in a small town.[7]

Likewise, it is apparent that any detailed compilation of statutory commands would operate to the disadvantage of the public. This is because such an enumeration would not reach unforeseen evasions by ingenious monopolistic minds. For example, a list of antisocial restraints in granting runs and clearances in the movie industry[8] could not readily be tailor-made to reach all abuses in the garment industry. Again, the condemnation of unreasonable contractual arrangements with prize fighters would not necessarily cover undesirable practices in the importation of perfume.[9] A comprehensive encyclopedia of prohibited restraints could be drafted to cover most industries, but even such a gargantuan catalog of possible antitrust sin would scarcely list all potential variations of irregular antitrust conduct. The problems experienced by our government in drafting NRA codes and Phase IV regulations with sufficient flexibility to reach the illicit, and exempt the licit, has taught us the dangers of rigid prescriptions in industrial prohibitions: "In thus divining that there was no limit to business ingenuity and legal gymnastics the Congress displayed much foresight."[10]

The second basic principle embodied in the antitrust laws is that the generality of their statutory language has necessitated the delegation to the Department of Justice, the Federal Trade Commission, and the courts a wide discretion in the interpretation and application of their competitive commands in specific cases.

The Antitrust Division of the Department of Justice and the Federal Trade Commission, with increasingly effective assistance from private litigants, initiate the proceedings invoking and seeking informative interpretations of the antitrust laws. It inevitably follows that in determining whether and how to frame complaints, and subsequently in seeking relief in accordance therewith, the division and

---

[4] See, for example, United States v. Concentrated Phosphate Export Association, Inc., 393 U.S. 199 (1968).
[5] United States v. Morgan, 118 F. Supp. 621 (S.D.N.Y. 1953).
[6] United States v. Aluminum Company of America, 148 F.2d 416 (2d Cir. 1945).
[7] United States v. Griffith, 334 U.S. 100 (1948).
[8] United States v. Paramount Pictures, Inc., 334 U.S. 131 (1948).
[9] Cf. United States v. International Boxing Club of New York, Inc., 348 U.S. 236 (1955) with United States v. Guerlain, Inc., 155 F.Supp. 77 (S.D.N.Y. 1957), *vacated mem.* 358 U.S. 915 (1958).
[10] Atlantic Refining Co. v. Federal Trade Commission, 381 U.S. 357, 367 (1965).

the commission substantially influence the developments in these laws. In particular, in shaping the controlling principles and resulting proscriptions of consent settlements, the two agencies prepare the way for the subsequent formulation by the courts of new antitrust rulings.

The courts, however, are ultimately responsible for the definitive interpretation and application of the antitrust laws. Our judiciary has been vested with a wide range of discretion in construing their statutory provisions, and in molding their remedies.[11] The government and private complainants may propose but the courts by independent adjudications will dispose of suggested applications of antitrust principles to industrial defendants: "In the antitrust field the courts have been accorded by common consent, an authority they have in no other branch of enacted law."[12]

These two fundamental principles, which give a rough unity to the provisions of our antitrust laws, can best be grasped when we turn to the specific wording of the individual statutes which embody these principles.

Present Restraints

The Sherman Antitrust Act, enacted in 1890, is the first congressional commandment embodying the competitive objective of and comprehensive delegation by our antitrust laws. The sections of this act prohibit unreasonable restraints upon and monopolization of trade, in broadly phrased terms comparable to those found in constitutional provisions.[13] They further delegate to the courts broad powers to interpret and apply their prohibitions, case by case, in civil and criminal actions brought by the Department of Justice and by private persons.

More specifically, section 1 of this act provides that

> [e]very contract, combination in the form of trust or otherwise, or conspiracy, in restraint of trade or commerce among the several States, or with foreign nations, is declared to be illegal. . . . [14]

This section, on its face, applies only if there is a "contract," "combination," or "conspiracy." This means that there must be some

---

[11] International Salt Co., Inc. v. United States, 332 U.S. 392 (1947).
[12] United States v. United Shoe Machinery Corp., 110 F. Supp. 295, 348 (D.Mass. 1953), aff'd, 347 U.S. 521 (1954).
[13] Appalachian Coals, Inc. v. United States, 288 U.S. 344 (1933).
[14] Sherman Antitrust Act sec. 1, 26 Stat. 209 (1890), as amended, 15 U.S.C.A. sec. 1 (Supp. I 1975).

cooperative relationship of two or more persons.[15] Next, the section is applicable only if the contract, combination, or conspiracy is a "restraint" of competition sufficiently grave to amount to a restraint of "trade" or "commerce."[16] That is to say, its provisions are relevant only if the facts—when weighed by the courts in the light of reason[17]—reveal either an unduly restraining effect upon trade or an intent so unduly to affect it.[18] Finally, the section applies solely where this contract, combination, or conspiracy is in restraint of "interstate" or "foreign" trade or commerce. These terms, however, have been construed, on the one hand, to reach restraints within a single city or state,[19] if they have a significant impact upon commerce between the states, and, on the other, to all transactions whose direct and substantial effect is to restrain our foreign trade.[20]

Section 2 of this act, in its turn, declares that

[e]very person who shall monopolize, or attempt to monopolize, or combine or conspire with any other person or persons, to monopolize any part of the trade or commerce among the several States, or with foreign nations, shall be deemed guilty of a felony . . . .[21]

This section, it will be noted, initially provides that no person shall "monopolize." It is interpreted thereby to prohibit the possession of power by anyone either to control the prices in, or to foreclose access to, trade or commerce, where such power has been obtained or maintained by methods evidencing the existence of an intent to exercise that power.[22] In short, the section condemns the intentional acquisition or enjoyment of dictatorial powers over the marketplace. This section then further condemns two other acts, namely, either an individual "attempt" by a single person, or a collective "combination" or "conspiracy" by two or more persons, to monopolize. By these additional prohibitions the section enables the courts to reach both joint and several actions whose objective is monopoly, whether or not monopoly is thereby in fact achieved.

The Sherman Act, by those two sections, thus reflects the first of the unifying principles of our antitrust laws in that it deals in com-

---

[15] Albrecht v. Herald Co., 390 U.S. 145 (1968).
[16] United States v. E. I. du Pont de Nemours & Company, 188 Fed.127 (C.C.D. Del. 1911).
[17] Standard Oil Company of New Jersey v. United States, 221 U.S. 1 (1911).
[18] United States v. American Tobacco Company, 221 U.S. 106 (1911).
[19] United States v. Employing Plasterers Association of Chicago, 347 U.S. 186 (1954); Mandeville Island Farms, Inc. v. American Crystal Sugar Co., 334 U.S. 219 (1948).
[20] United States v. Aluminum Company of America, 148 F.2d 416 (2d Cir. 1945).
[21] Sherman Antitrust Act sec. 2, 26 Stat. 209 (1890), as amended, 15 U.S.C.A. sec. 2 (Supp. I 1975).
[22] American Tobacco Co. v. United States, 328 U.S. 781 (1946); Otter Tail Power Co. v. United States, 410 U.S. 366 (1973).

prehensive fashion with the subject of actual (in other words, presently existing) trade restraints. The first section deals with "restraint," while the second goes after the end product of restraint, namely, "monopolization." The one forbids joint action, whereas the other proscribes both individual and joint activity. Collectively they reach "every" transaction and "every" person having the purpose or effect of imposing undue, provable restrictions upon competition in interstate or foreign trade.[23]

The Sherman Act then further reveals the second unifying antitrust principle by its delegation to the courts of power to determine, over the years, the meaning and application of its prohibitions. The discretion of the judiciary in deciding in the light of reason what is and is not a forbidden restraint is thereby limited by little more than the courts' self-restraint: "The prohibitions of the Sherman Act were not stated in terms of precision or of crystal clarity and the Act itself does not define them. In consequence of the vagueness of its language . . . the courts have been left to give content to the statute . . . ."[24]

Probable Restraints

Two subsequently enacted statutes, namely, the Clayton Act in 1914 and the Robinson-Patman Act in 1936, also seek to ensure to us a competitive economy by comprehensive delegation of broad administrative powers to agencies and courts. The sections of these acts, however, are not directed at conduct which has materialized into restraints of trade, as in the Sherman Act, but at certain practices which manifest a substantial probability of becoming such restraints. Congress nevertheless here also has stated its objective of promoting competition by generally phrased prohibitions, whose meaning must be developed case by case in proceedings brought in the courts and before the Federal Trade Commission.

Section 2 of the Clayton Act (which was amended by and is now identical with section 1 of the Robinson-Patman Act) declares that it is unlawful for any person, in interstate or foreign commerce, to discriminate in price between purchasers of commodities of like grade and quality sold for use, consumption, or resale within the United States and its territories

> where the effect of such discrimination may be substantially
> to lessen competition or tend to create a monopoly in any line
> of commerce, or to injure, destroy, or prevent competition

---

[23] United States v. South-Eastern Underwriters Association, 322 U.S. 533 (1944).
[24] Apex Hosiery Co. v. Leader, 310 U.S. 469, 489 (1940).

9

with any person who either grants or knowingly receives the benefit of such discrimination, or with customers of either of them . . . .[25]

The section, by this prohibition, forbids a seller in interstate commerce to "discriminate" (that is, to differentiate) in price.[26] It condemns such a differentiation in price, however, only where the discriminatory prices are embodied in sales of the same or similar commodities[27] to two or more "purchasers," and where the effect of such discriminatory prices "may be" substantially to lessen competition in a line of commerce or with specified persons. In addition, two other provisos of the section permit such discrimination if it is justified by cost savings[28] or by the necessity to meet in good faith[29] the equally low prices of a competitor.[30]

The section then continues, in further subsections, to provide that sellers and buyers may not directly or indirectly pay to each other "brokerage,"[31] and to specify that sellers may neither pay allowances for, nor themselves furnish, promotional "services or facilities," unless all purchasers (competing in the resale of the former's commodities) are offered "proportionally" similar or comparable treatment.[32] Other supplemental provisions then make the buyer, as well as the seller, liable for unlawful price discrimination under certain circumstances[33] and provide criminal sanctions for a variety of discriminatory and predatory pricing practices.[34]

Section 3 of the Clayton Act, in its turn, provides that it shall be unlawful for any person, in interstate or foreign commerce, to lease or sell commodities for use, consumption, or resale within the United States or its territories, or to charge a price therefor

on the condition, agreement or understanding that the lessee or purchaser thereof shall not use or deal in the goods . . . or other commodities of a competitor or competitors of the lessor or seller where the effect of such lease, sale, or

---

[25] Robinson-Patman Price Discrimination Act sec. 1, 49 Stat. 1526 (1936), 15 U.S.C.A. sec. 13 (1970).

[26] Gulf Oil Corp. v. Copp Paving Co., 95 S. Ct. 392 (1974); Federal Trade Commission v. Anheuser-Busch, Inc., 363 U.S. 536 (1960); see also, 289 F.2d 835 (7th Cir. 1961).

[27] Federal Trade Commission v. Borden Co., 383 U.S. 637 (1966).

[28] Federal Trade Commission, Advisory Committee on Cost Justification, *Report to the Federal Trade Commission* (1956). See also United States v. Borden Co., 370 U.S. 460 (1962).

[29] Federal Trade Commission v. A. E. Staley Mfg. Co., 324 U.S. 746 (1945).

[30] Standard Oil Co. v. Federal Trade Commission, 340 U.S. 231 (1951); Federal Trade Commission v. Sun Oil Co., 371 U.S. 505 (1963).

[31] Federal Trade Commission v. Henry Broch & Co., 363 U.S. 166 (1960).

[32] Federal Trade Commission v. Simplicity Pattern Co., Inc., 360 U.S. 55 (1959).

[33] Federal Trade Commission v. Fred Meyer, Inc., 390 U.S. 341 (1968).

[34] United States v. National Dairy Prods. Corp., 372 U.S. 29 (1963).

contract for sale or such condition, agreement or understanding may be to substantially lessen competition or tend to create a monopoly in any line of commerce.[35]

At the outset it will be noted that this section is concerned with exclusive-dealing arrangements, total-requirement obligations, and so-called tying arrangements (under which commodities are made available only upon the condition that other and differing commodities are taken) when contained in "leases" and "sales."[36] It does not affect simple refusals to sell or ordinary agency arrangements.[37] It will be further observed that this section applies to these restrictive contractual arrangements solely if their provisions operate to lease or sell commodities[38] in a manner to require the lessee or purchaser to refrain from doing business with a "competitor" of the lessor or vendor. Finally, somewhat in the manner of section 2, the section forbids such contractual arrangements only if under all the circumstances,[39] their probable effect "may be" substantially to lessen competition or to tend to create a monopoly.[40] Thus it does not preclude the imposition of an obligation that a lessee or purchaser conform to reasonable standards of quality[41] and fair competition.[42]

Section 7 of the Clayton Act, thereafter, deals with corporate acquisitions and mergers. As amended in 1950 (by the Celler-Kefauver Act), this section, generally speaking, prohibits the acquisition by a corporation of

the whole or any part of the stock or . . . assets of another corporation engaged also in commerce, where in any line of commerce in any section of the country, the effect of such acquisition may be substantially to lessen competition, or to tend to create a monopoly.[43]

The provisions of this section initially apply to the acquisition by one corporation of the "stock" or "assets" of another corporation engaged in the interstate or foreign commerce of this country, whether the respective corporations do or do not compete.[44] The section thereby exempts from its application those acquisitions in which

---

[35] Clayton Act sec. 3, 38 Stat. 731 (1914), 15 U.S.C.A. sec. 14 (1970).
[36] Standard Oil Company of California v. United States, 337 U.S. 293 (1949).
[37] Federal Trade Commission v. Curtis Publishing Company, 260 U.S. 568 (1923).
[38] Cf. Times-Picayune Publishing Co. v. United States, 345 U.S. 594 (1953).
[39] Tampa Electric Co. v. Nashville Coal Co., 365 U.S. 320 (1961).
[40] Standard Fashion Co. v. Magrane-Houston Co., 258 U.S. 346 (1922).
[41] See International Salt Co., Inc. v. United States, 332 U.S. 392 (1947).
[42] Federal Trade Commission v. Sinclair Refining Company, 261 U.S. 463 (1923).
[43] Clayton Act sec. 7, 38 Stat. 731 (1914), as amended, 15 U.S.C.A. sec. 18 (1970).
[44] United States v. E. I. du Pont de Nemours & Company, 353 U.S. 586 (1957).

one of the two parties is an individual or partnership or the acquired corporation is not engaged in interstate or foreign commerce. The section then proceeds to grant two further exemptions, namely where an acquisition of assets is made by a corporation not subject to the jurisdiction of the Federal Trade Commission,[45] or an acquisition of stock is made solely for the purpose of investment and therefore is not used to restrain trade.[46] Finally, the section (much as in the case of its predecessors) does not condemn any such transaction unless its probable effect "may be" substantially to lessen competition or tend to create a monopoly in a line of commerce in some section of the country.[47]

In summary, these sections (and certain others dealing with such subjects as interlocking directorates),[48] like the provisions of the Sherman Act, embody the first unifying principle of our antitrust laws in that they collectively proscribe additional private restraints which are believed to endanger our competitive economy. Their aim, however, is to forestall probable threats to, rather than eradicate actual restraints of, competition in this economy. In addition, by the generality of their language, they similarly provide for a substantial delegation of power to our administrative agencies and the judiciary. As candidly conceded in a lower court ruling, "Few Clayton Act cases are simple. Seldom is the Court without doubt in its decision even though it does not say so."[49]

Unfair Restraints

Finally, the Federal Trade Commission Act, originally enacted in 1914 and substantially amended in 1938, 1973, and 1975, supplements the Sherman and Clayton Acts in fostering competition with sweeping prohibitions of unfair methods, acts, and practices. It further provides that these prohibitions are to be interpreted and enforced in administrative proceedings brought by and before the Federal Trade Commission subject to review by the courts. Section 5 of the act, in part, provides that:

---

[45] But cf. United States v. Philadelphia Nat'l Bank, 374 U.S. 321 (1963).

[46] Pennsylvania R. Co. v. Interstate Commerce Commission, 66 F.2d 37 (3d Cir. 1933), aff'd, 291 U.S. 651 (1934). But cf. Hamilton Watch Co. v. Benrus Watch Co., Inc., 206 F.2d 738 (2d Cir. 1953).

[47] United States v. General Dynamics Corp., 415 U.S. 486 (1974).

[48] See, for example, United States v. Sears, Roebuck & Co., 111 F. Supp. 614 (S.D.N.Y. 1953).

[49] United States v. Brown Shoe Company, Inc., CCH 1956 Trade Cases para. 68,244 (E.D. Mo. 1956), judgment accord. 179 F. Supp. 721 (E.D. Mo. 1959); aff'd 370 U.S. 294 (1962).

[u]nfair methods of competition in or affecting commerce, and unfair or deceptive acts or practices in or affecting commerce, are declared unlawful.[50]

The initial language of this section (while not technically defined by Congress as an antitrust law) in reality overlaps and embraces the subject matter of the other antitrust laws. This is because its prohibition of "unfair methods of competition" is construed to condemn unreasonable restraints[51] in or affecting interstate and foreign trade.[52] The subsequent words of the section, however, in outlawing "unfair or deceptive acts or practices," are interpreted to go beyond the other antitrust laws and to reach all "unfair" practices in or affecting such commerce, whether or not they are "methods of competition."[53] It follows, therefore, that the section initially accords to the commission and courts the power to prohibit the present and potential trade restraints which are proscribed by the Sherman and Clayton Acts, as, for example, price fixing[54] and boycotts.[55] It likewise follows, however, that the thrust of the section goes even deeper, for it also authorizes the commission to proceed against—as "unfair"— other antisocial business conduct,[56] such as misrepresentation[57] and the utilization of lotteries to sell goods.[58] In this sense, therefore, the Federal Trade Commission Act may be viewed as reaching even further than the preceding antitrust laws.[59]

The prohibitions of this act, nevertheless, as in the case of the other statutes, are likewise phrased in general terms to be interpreted and clarified, proceeding by proceeding, by the commission and courts. The act therefore conforms, similarly, to our two-fold statutory pattern, previously described, of a sweeping prohibition of private practices deemed to endanger our economy, and an equally sweeping delegation of discretion to the ultimate interpreters of this act:

> In a broad delegation of power it empowers the Commission, in the first instance, to determine whether a method of com-

---

[50] Federal Trade Commission Act sec. 5, 38 Stat. 719 (1914), 15 U.S.C.A. sec. 45 (Supp. I 1975).
[51] Federal Trade Commission v. Cement Institute, 333 U.S. 683 (1948).
[52] The 1975 amendment of section 5, as quoted above, has overruled Federal Trade Commission v. Bunte Brothers, Inc., 312 U.S. 349 (1941).
[53] Federal Trade Commission v. Sperry & Hutchinson Co., 405 U.S. 233 (1972).
[54] Federal Trade Commission v. Pacific States Paper Trade Association, 273 U.S. 52 (1927).
[55] Fashion Originators' Guild of America, Inc. v. Federal Trade Commission, 312 U.S. 457 (1941).
[56] Federal Trade Commission v. Gratz, 253 U.S. 421 (1920).
[57] Federal Trade Commission v. Mary Carter Paint Co., 382 U.S. 46 (1965).
[58] Federal Trade Commission v. R. F. Keppel & Bro., Inc., 291 U.S. 304 (1934).
[59] Federal Trade Commission v. Brown Shoe Co., 384 U.S. 316 (1966).

petition or the act or practice complained of is unfair. The Congress intentionally left development of the term "unfair" to the Commission rather than attempting to define the many and variable unfair practices which prevail in commerce.[60]

Further analysis of these statutes would, of course, reveal additional distinctions of interest to the practicing lawyer. This brief summary, however, should suffice to disclose to the lay eye that, by this legislation, Congress has placed in the custody of the courts what amounts to a three-headed Cerberus to guard our competitive economy from the encroachment of undesirable private restraints. Its "Sherman" head is instructed to watch for present dangers to this economy; its "Clayton" (including Robinson-Patman) head is directed to look for probable threats; and its "commission" head has a roving mission to detect unfair hazards. The courts, however, with the advice and consent of public and private plaintiffs, are given final authority to determine when, where, and how this antitrust guardian is to be unleashed against any such intruding restraints which endanger that free economy.

---

[60] Atlantic Refining Co. v. Federal Trade Commission, 381 U.S. 357, 367 (1965).

3

THE INTERPRETATION OF THE ANTITRUST LAWS

Judicial Principles

The judicial opinions interpreting the statutes in this field of law are most readily understood by the lay reader if it is recognized that these rulings, similarly, have conformed to two unifying principles.

The first basic principle reflected in these opinions is that the courts, in exercising their delegated power to construe the general provisions of the antitrust laws, have proceeded through the process of interpretation to supplement—and to implement—this vaguely phrased legislation with more specific judicial legislation. As previously explained, Congress by these laws has imposed upon the courts the task of bringing its competitive commands down from Capitol Hill and inscribing them, case by case, in the tablets of court records. This sweeping delegation of authority has thereby forced the legislative quill into the—at times not unreceptive—judicial hand: "the courts have been given by Congress wide powers in monopoly regulation. The very broadness of terms such as restraint of trade, substantial competition and purpose to monopolize have placed upon courts the responsibility to . . . avoid the evils at which Congress aimed."[1]

This legislative role of the courts has inevitably led to the uncertainty of past precedent in this field of law. Just as one Congress has not been able to bind irrevocably a subsequent Congress, so the early courts in their antitrust rulings have not succeeded in controlling later courts. The judicial legislation of one decade[2] has at times been drastically amended in another.[3] A corporation informed in one

---

[1] United States v. Columbia Steel Co., 334 U.S. 495, 526 (1948).
[2] United States v. Colgate & Company, 250 U.S. 300 (1919).
[3] United States v. Parke, Davis & Co., 362 U.S. 29 (1960); 365 U.S. 125 (1961).

proceeding that a practice is lawful[4] may receive totally contrary instructions in subsequent litigation.[5]

This legislative process in the functioning of our courts has also resulted in the continuous appearance of new precedents. As the national economy has expanded, our courts have been forced to determine whether local business transactions, previously considered to be beyond the scope of the laws, should or should not be subject under modern conditions to interstate antitrust principles.[6] In like fashion, differences in the structures and performances of industries and between members of these industries have continuously presented new problems, which have not been capable of resolution by an existing pat formula, but have required solution by *sui generis* rulings.[7] The generality of the antitrust laws has both necessitated, and made possible, this flexible application: "Because the Act is couched in broad terms, it is adaptable to the changing types of commercial production and distribution that have evolved since its passage."[8]

The second principle reflected in these opinions is that the courts, in thus implementing the general commands of congressional legislation with specific rulings in judicial legislation, have explored the reasons underlying the desire of Congress to prohibit private restraints adversely affecting a competitive economy, and have attempted to conform their own supplementary trade regulations to these antecedent congressional reasons. They have therefore studied carefully the hearings, reports, and debates of our federal legislators. In the course of this judicial research, the courts have determined that Congress has sought to achieve—through prohibiting restraints threatening a competitive economy—the three-fold blessings of material prosperity, political democracy, and an ethical society. The courts, accordingly, have conscientiously recognized and consistently endeavored to reflect each of these three congressional reasons for our antitrust laws in evolving their more detailed judicial regulations. They have emphasized "the importance of giving hospitable scope to Congressional purpose even when meticulous words are lacking."[9]

These three congressional reasons have, at times, clashed. On such an occasion, it naturally follows, the courts have found it necessary to choose between these conflicting economic, political, and

---

[4] United States v. United Shoe Machinery Company of New Jersey, 247 U.S. 32 (1918).
[5] United States v. United Shoe Machinery Corp., 110 F. Supp. 295 (D. Mass. 1953), *aff'd*, 347 U.S. 521 (1954).
[6] United States v. South-Eastern Underwriters Association, 322 U.S. 533 (1944).
[7] United States v. Jerrold Electronics Corporation, 187 F. Supp. 545 (E.D. Pa. 1960), *aff'd*, 365 U.S. 567 (1961).
[8] United States v. E. I. du Pont de Nemours & Company, 351 U.S. 377, 386 (1956).
[9] United States v. Hutcheson, 312 U.S. 219, 235 (1941); *accord*, Minnesota Mining and Manufacturing Co. v. New Jersey Wood Finishing Co., 381 U.S. 311 (1965).

ethical reasons and, in the course of resolving this conflict, occasionally to hand down inconsistent rulings. Thus, in a case involving cellophane, an economic analysis by the courts resulted in a broad definition of the market (vindicating conduct of a defendant found to have a small share of this large market), whereas shortly afterwards, in another case involving paint and fabrics, an essentially political approach was responsible for a narrow market definition (condemning the same defendant for possessing a large share in this small market).[10] The courts have sought as best they can to reconcile these economic, political, and ethical motivations of Congress, but they have found it impossible at times to refine away all differences. As these underlying legislative reasons are so influential in the evolution by the courts of their antitrust rulings, they bear further analysis.

Economic Reasons

It is well known that Congress enacted the antitrust laws in part because of its belief that a competitive economy would best ensure a prosperous economy. Our legislative fathers agreed with Aristotle that "it is best to have property private" because "each person will labor to improve his own private property" and thereby increase the aggregate industrial wealth (while "what is common to many is least taken care of").[11] But they also agreed with Adam Smith that private enterprise must be guided by the "invisible hand" of competition, in order to be sure that it thereby serves society.[12] They were convinced that the development of our nation's resources could not safely be left to the personal judgment either of business barons or of public planners. They felt, rather, that the future of our economy should be determined by the impersonal judgment of the marketplace.[13] They sought, therefore, to require commerce in goods and services to stand the cold test of competition and thereby to avoid the control of prices, the restriction of production, and other evils arising from undue limitation of competitive conditions.[14] The interaction of competitive forces was thought to advance most effectively our material progress.[15]

The courts in their opinions, accordingly, have endeavored to

[10] Compare United States v. E. I. du Pont de Nemours & Company, 351 U.S. 377 (1956) with United States v. E. I. du Pont de Nemours & Company, 353 U.S. 586 (1957).
[11] Aristotle, *The Politics of Aristotle: A Treatise on Government*, trans. William Ellis, ed. Ernest Rhys, Everyman's Library (London: T. N. Dent & Sons, Ltd., 1947) (New York: E. P. Dutton & Co., 1947), pp. 29, 33–34.
[12] Adam Smith, *The Wealth of Nations* (New York: Modern Library Giants, 1937), p. 423.
[13] Times-Picayune Publishing Co. v. United States, 345 U.S. 594 (1953).
[14] Standard Oil Company of New Jersey v. United States, 221 U.S. 1 (1911).
[15] Northern Pacific Railway Company v. United States, 356 U.S. 1 (1958).

conform their rulings to this underlying economic motivation of our legislative draftsmen. They have emphasized (as, for example, with respect to our basic Sherman Act) "the Sherman Law and the judicial decisions interpreting it are based upon the assumption that the public interest is best protected from the evils of monopoly and price control by the maintenance of competition."[16]

On the one hand, therefore, the courts in supplementing the antitrust laws with specific judicial rulings have held that those who venture their time, skill, and capital in commerce without engaging in competitive abuses should be accorded substantial freedom of action.[17] Thus congressional prohibitions of "restraint" and "monopoly" have been construed to permit commercial enterprises to enjoy large[18] and integrated[19] corporate structures. Again, ambiguous statutory limitations upon "discrimination" have been interpreted to contemplate competition for survival between sellers, in preference to cartels with security for buyers.[20] The objective of these laws has been declared to be workable competition, as distinguished from some utopia of perfect competition.[21]

On the other hand, however, the courts have moved with Draconic severity against those who have been found to have abused this freedom of action to the detriment of a competitive economy. Executives who have destroyed competition by fixing prices and allocating business have been fined and sent to jail;[22] corporate monopolizers have been divested of their property;[23] unjustified discrimination between competing customers has been enjoined;[24] undue control over small dealers by a network of consignment and exclusive dealing requirements has been outlawed;[25] and substantial acquisitions of solvent competitors[26] and customers[27] have been condemned.

---

[16] United States v. Trenton Potteries Company, 273 U.S. 392, 397 (1927).

[17] Federal Trade Commission v. Sinclair Refining Company, 261 U.S. 463 (1923).

[18] United States v. E. I. du Pont de Nemours & Company, 351 U.S. 377 (1956).

[19] United States v. Columbia Steel Co., 334 U.S. 495 (1948).

[20] Standard Oil Co. v. Federal Trade Commission, 340 U.S. 231 (1951).

[21] United States v. Aluminum Company of America, 91 F. Supp. 333 (S.D.N.Y. 1950).

[22] United States v. McDonough Co., 180 F. Supp. 511 (S.D. Ohio 1959); United States v. Westinghouse Electric Corp., CCH Transfer Binder, *U.S. Antitrust Cases Summaries, 1957–1961*, Case 1496, et al. (1960–61).

[23] United States v. International Boxing Club of New York, Inc., 348 U.S. 236 (1955); United States v. Paramount Pictures, Inc., 85 F. Supp. 881 (S.D.N.Y. 1949).

[24] Federal Trade Commission v. Morton Salt Co., 334 U.S. 37 (1948); Federal Trade Commission v. Cement Institute, 333 U.S. 683 (1948).

[25] Simpson v. Union Oil Co., 377 U.S. 13 (1964); Standard Oil Company of California v. United States, 337 U.S. 293 (1949).

[26] United States v. Aluminum Co. of America, 377 U.S. 271 (1964); United States v. Philadelphia Nat'l Bank, 374 U.S. 321 (1963).

[27] Brown Shoe Co. v. United States, 370 U.S. 294 (1962); United States v. E. I. du Pont de Nemours & Company, 353 U.S. 586 (1957).

18

Political Reasons

It is also well known that Congress drafted the various antitrust laws in part because of its political conviction that a competitive economy would best promote a democratic society. These laws were desired by Congress, not only because a competitive economy was believed to promote our material prosperity, but also because such competition was thought to be most conducive to preserving a Jeffersonian society of many independent, small businessmen. Thus the original Sherman Act was enacted in an era of trusts and combinations which had threatened to control the political life of our nation.[28] One of the purposes of this statute, accordingly, was to guard our country from the power of rapidly accumulating individual and corporate wealth.[29] As Senator Sherman emphasized—in denouncing concentration of economic wealth—if we in this country will not endure a king or an emperor, "we should not submit to an autocrat of trade."[30] Again, in subsequent decades, the Clayton, Robinson-Patman, and Federal Trade Commission Acts were, in substantial measure, passed in order to check the power of large buying[31] and selling[32] organizations, to halt the trend toward industrial concentration,[33] and to stop in their incipiency acts and practices which, when full blown, would result in anticompetitive restraints and monopoly[34]: "Throughout the history of these statutes it has been constantly assumed that one of their purposes was to perpetuate and preserve, for its own sake and in spite of possible cost, an organization of industry in small units which can effectively compete with each other."[35]

The courts in their supplementary opinions, therefore, have also been influenced by this political purpose of Congress. The judiciary has been increasingly critical of the large, and concerned for the small, businessman. For example, while they continue to recognize that size by itself does not violate the law, they have repeatedly condemned the use of size to obtain an undue competitive advantage.[36] They have sought to ensure that the large and the small buyers who resell at the same functional level start on an equal competitive footing.[37] In contrast, they have been prompt to protect the small merchant, even

---

[28] Apex Hosiery Co. v. Leader, 310 U.S. 469 (1940).
[29] Standard Oil Company of New Jersey v. United States, 221 U.S. 1 (1911).
[30] *Congressional Record*, 21st Cong., 1st sess., 1890, p. 2457.
[31] Federal Trade Commission v. Henry Broch & Co., 363 U.S. 166 (1960).
[32] Standard Oil Company of California v. United States, 337 U.S. 293 (1949).
[33] United States v. Bethlehem Steel Corporation, 168 F. Supp. 576 (S.D.N.Y. 1958).
[34] Federal Trade Commission v. Motion Picture Advertising Service Co., Inc., 344 U.S. 392 (1953).
[35] United States v. Aluminum Company of America, 148 F.2d 416, 429 (2d Cir. 1945).
[36] Otter Tail Power Co. v. United States, 410 U.S. 366 (1973).
[37] Federal Trade Commission v. Sun Oil Co., 371 U.S. 505 (1963).

where his business is so minor that his destruction would make little difference to our economy.[38]

In their rulings, it follows, our courts have frequently judged restraints more strictly where participated in by a large company than where attempted by a small one. Thus, a company enjoying a large share of a market has been held to have violated the antitrust laws when it has engaged in the practices of leasing machines[39] and of constructing new production facilities;[40] but no small company has, to date, been condemned for participating in these normal commercial activities. Again, large companies have been enjoined from licensing patents on condition that their licensees grant back comparable licenses, but a small company has been permitted to do so.[41] Likewise, a merger of large companies has been ruled to be more vulnerable than a combination of small ones.[42] The uniform approach of the courts toward small companies has been to protect, preserve, and promote their freedom of action wherever possible.

The courts have recognized, however, that the political desirability of small units must nevertheless be subordinate to, and consistent with, the competitive spirit of the antitrust laws. Early in the history of these statutes the Supreme Court pointed out that even practices adopted by industry in order to protect the small retailer, where unduly restrictive of trade, must be outlawed in deference to the basic antitrust objective of a competitive economy.[43]

Ethical Reasons

It is less widely understood in industrial circles that Congress, in enacting the antitrust laws, likewise sought to establish ethical standards for the conduct of business. For example, an underlying motivation for the Sherman Act was a desire to make it possible for businessmen to engage in fair competition, without exclusion from or coercion in the marketplace by combinations and monopolies.[44] In particular, the Federal Trade Commission Act was subsequently

---

[38] Klor's, Inc. v. Broadway-Hale Stores, Inc., 359 U.S. 207 (1959), and Radiant Burners, Inc. v. Peoples Gas Light & Coke Co., 364 U.S. 656 (1961).
[39] United States v. United Shoe Machinery Corp., 110 F. Supp. 295 (D.Mass 1953), aff'd, 347 U.S. 521 (1954).
[40] United States v. Aluminum Company of America, 148 F.2d 416 (2d Cir. 1945).
[41] Cf. United States v. General Electric Co., 80 F. Supp. 989 (S.D.N.Y. 1948), and United States v. General Electric Co., 82 F. Supp. 753 (D.N.J. 1949), with Transparent-Wrap Machine Corp. v. Stokes & Smith Co., 329 U.S. 637 (1947).
[42] Cf. United States v. Bethlehem Steel Corp., 168 F. Supp. 576 (S.D.N.Y. 1958), with United States v. Republic Steel Corp., 11 F. Supp. 117 (N.D. Ohio 1935).
[43] Eastern States Retail Lumber Dealers' Association v. United States, 234 U.S. 600 (1914); accord, United States v. Topco Associates, Inc., 405 U.S. 596 (1972).
[44] United States v. E. I. du Pont de Nemours & Company, 351 U.S. 377 (1956).

enacted in order to ensure that the ethical businessman was not placed at an unfair disadvantage in competing with the unscrupulous merchant.[45]

Indeed, the latter act was in turn amended to extend its protection to consumers as well as competitors victimized by unfair practices: "Congress amended the Act in 1938 to include unfair or deceptive acts or practices in commerce—a significant amendment showing Congress' concern for consumers as well as for competitors."[46]

In deference to this ethical objective of Congress, accordingly, the courts have tended to deal more harshly with the deliberate violator who consciously flouts the provisions of the antitrust laws, than with the businessman who seeks in good faith to comply with their commands. Thus price cutting engaged in with the specific intent to destroy competition is held to be unlawful, while similar action in furtherance of a legitimate commercial objective is approved.[47] Again, an acquisition by an empire builder of a healthy competitor is condemned, whereas a defensive merger of a small or failing company is permitted.[48]

In passing judgment on individual businessmen, the issue of good or bad motives is particularly relevant. A corporate executive who knowingly authorizes an illegal act can expect little sympathy,[49] but one who has sought to comply with the law may successfully plead good faith in mitigation of penalties which otherwise might be imposed.[50]

The courts have likewise sought to promote and upgrade fair dealings between businessmen. Prohibition by the Federal Trade Commission of unethical practices in the business community has increasingly been upheld.[51] Cooperative action by industrial organizations to foster fair competitive opportunities has, to a limited degree, been encouraged.[52] For similar reasons, misuse of the antitrust laws by private litigants to avoid contractual obligations, entered into without coercion, has been discouraged.[53] But these ethical rulings, needless to say, have been directed toward ensuring the continuance of competition—not its suppression. Just as the courts hold that practices seeking to protect the small businessman may violate the

---

45 Federal Trade Commission v. R. F. Keppel & Bro., Inc., 291 U.S. 304 (1934).
46 Federal Trade Commission v. Colgate-Palmolive Co., 380 U.S. 374, 384 (1965).
47 United States v. National Dairy Prods. Corp., 372 U.S. 29 (1963).
48 Brown Shoe Co. v. United States, 370 U.S. 294 (1962).
49 United States v. Wise, 370 U.S. 405 (1962).
50 United States v. W. T. Grant Co., 345 U.S. 629, 633 (1953); United States v. Saul J. Karns, 1963 Trade Cas. para. 70,950 (S.D.N.Y. 1963).
51 Federal Trade Commission v. Sperry & Hutchinson Co., 405 U.S. 233 (1972).
52 Sugar Institute, Inc. v. United States, 297 U.S. 553 (1936).
53 Bruce's Juices, Inc. v. American Can Co., 330 U.S. 743 (1947), and Kelley v. Kosuga, 358 U.S. 516 (1959).

antitrust laws, so likewise they rule that action to improve the business ethics of industry "would not justify . . . combining together to regulate and restrain interstate commerce in violation of federal law."[54]

In short, the courts—in supplementing the antitrust laws with judicial interpretation—have respected the congressional intent underlying the general prohibitions of private restraints, and have endeavored to conform to this intent in exercising their delegated powers. Their rulings have consistently sought to follow the mainstream of statutory language back to its congressional source, and to reflect faithfully the three legislative wellsprings from which this statutory language has gushed forth. The underlying objective of their opinions—paralleling the general direction of the antitrust current—has ever been to preserve, protect, and promote our competitive economy. The pulsating and circuitous eddies of their resulting rulings have generally responded to the economic, political, and ethical views of our elected representatives.

---

[54] Fashion Originators' Guild of America, Inc. v. Federal Trade Commission, 312 U.S. 457, 468 (1941).

4

THE APPLICATION OF THE ANTITRUST LAWS

Factual Investigation

It is now necessary to leave the general statutory words and supplementary judicial construction of our antitrust laws and to consider their practical application. These laws, of course, do not operate in a vacuum. They must be reduced to concrete rulings directed, case by case, to specific industries and to particular members of these industries.

The businessman can best comprehend how these laws are applied by judicial construction if he assumes that a court approaches each antitrust case much like a physician about to treat a patient. The judge possesses certain professional knowledge of the statutory language and judicial principles to assist him in prescribing remedies for commercial illness. He must, however, study carefully the special symptoms of each individual and corporate patient, in each proceeding, before he can intelligently decide whether to send the patient happily home, or—alternatively—to curtail questionable activities by injunctions, to perform the surgical operation of divestiture, to prescribe costly payment of fines and damages, and/or to direct enforced rest in a government institution.

The commercial facts in such a proceeding may, on occasion, reveal a competitive restraint of a nature prohibited on its face by the statutory language of one or more of the three sets of antitrust laws above reviewed such as, for example, an agreement between competitors which establishes the prices in, or excludes others from, the market. In this event the court will condemn the conduct out of hand as an indefensible, or per se, violation of these laws. There is, of course, little need for going beyond the congressional language of the statutes when a transaction discloses price fixing, boycotting, or tie-in practices because "[w]hile the Court has utilized the 'rule of reason' in evaluating the legality of most restraints alleged to be violative of the Sherman Act, it has also developed the doctrine that certain business relationships are *per se* violations of the Act without regard to a consideration of their reasonableness."[1]

The industrial symptoms normally reveal, however, at most a competitive restraint of an ambiguous nature. In this event, the court may not safely prescribe any per se or "patent medicine" remedy, but must evaluate these ambiguous facts in the light of the three congressional reasons above discussed for desiring a competitive economy. In such a case "[t]o determine . . . [antitrust legality] the court must ordinarily consider the facts peculiar to the business to which the restraint is applied; its condition before and after the restraint was imposed; the nature of the restraint, and its effect, actual or probable."[2]

It follows, therefore, that the judicial process of applying the antitrust laws in an individual proceeding usually requires factual as well as legal research. Initially, the facts relevant to the nature of the restraint at issue must be determined. Once the relevant facts are segregated, however, they must be analyzed in the light of the economic, political, and ethical reasons underlying these laws. Thus, the judicial tests for appraising alleged present, probable, and unfair restraints revealed by these facts will vary by reason of the differences in the language of the applicable statutes. Three central aspects of any restraint are customarily held to be of particular significance in such an analysis, namely (1) the purpose of the restraint, (2) its effect, and (3) who is involved.

The "purpose" of an alleged restraint is the first of these critical facts. This subjective fact is important because the intent of the parties helps to guide the courts as they implement the reasons of Congress for enacting the antitrust laws. Thus, an intent by a defendant to promote the overall congressional objective of a competitive economy will assist a court in sympathetically evaluating the economic necessity for, and industrial impact of, challenged action.[3] Again, such a purpose will influence both judge and jury on ethical grounds to resolve doubts in favor of the defendant.[4] Accordingly, from the outset in this field of law the courts have sought to determine whether the purpose of a defendant was or was not to achieve the

---

[1] United States v. Topco Associates, Inc., 405 U.S. 596, 607 (1972).
[2] Chicago Board of Trade v. United States, 246 U.S. 231, 238 (1918).
[3] Appalachian Coals, Inc. v. United States, 288 U.S. 344 (1933).
[4] Compare Tampa Electric Co. v. Nashville Coal Co., 365 U.S. 320 (1961) with Northern Pacific Railway Company v. United States, 356 U.S. 1 (1958).

benefits desired by society from competition.[5] In particular, a deliberate plan by a defendant to flout the competitive commands of these laws will be deemed by the courts to convert an otherwise ambiguous conduct into a prohibited restraint, repugnant equally to the economic and moral objectives of the legislative draftsmen.[6]

The "effect" of the alleged restraint is the second of these critical facts. An objective inquiry into the result of challenged action is pertinent particularly to the economic and political convictions of Congress underlying these laws. The courts therefore probe searchingly into the resulting impact of an alleged restraint upon the productivity of, and the number of competitors in, the market. Thus, the courts tend to approve the action of a defendant where it has resulted in effective competition that has been economically productive of consumer benefits.[7] In this event they tend to give less weight to the political issue of whether there have been few or many competitors who have contributed to these benefits[8] or to the ethical question of their moral behavior.[9] On the other hand, when a restraint has contributed few, if any, consumer benefits and has limited the number of competitors, by foreclosing access to the market, the political desirability of a free economy has resulted in the condemnation of the restraint.[10]

The third key fact is "who." It is true that the statutory language and competitive objective of our antitrust laws apply equally to all persons. It is also true, however, that the underlying economic, political, and ethical reasons of Congress in drafting these statutes and in desiring competition have carefully differentiated between large and small business. Thus, congressional hearings have stressed that the economic significance of a competitor's decision often increases in rough proportion to the size of the capital resources of that competitor. Again, our elected representatives have been keenly aware that the large corporation tends to be feared and the small to be favored politically in the voting booth. Finally, our moral reflexes both within and without legislative halls have cautioned the powerful national organization to "pick on someone his own size." The courts, therefore, have also been noticeably influenced by the relative strength of the parties. Thus the Supreme Court—in refusing to condemn certain vertical restraints of trade until it knew more of the purpose and effect

[5] United States v. Addyston Pipe & Steel Co., 85 Fed. 271 (6th Cir. 1898), aff'd, 175 U.S. 211 (1899).
[6] Swift & Company v. United States, 196 U.S. 375 (1905).
[7] United States v. E. I. du Pont de Nemours & Company, 351 U.S. 377 (1956).
[8] United States v. National Lead Co., 332 U.S. 319 (1947).
[9] Eastern Railroad Presidents Conference v. Noerr Motor Freight, Inc., 365 U.S. 127 (1961).
[10] International Salt Co., Inc. v. United States, 332 U.S. 392 (1947).

of the challenged transactions—stressed that it might look favorably on these restraints if they were essential for the survival of a small company, but would take a dim view of them if, instead, they were dangerous practices of a large one.[11] A favorite story in antitrust circles is that of the prosecutor who paused after explaining in his opening statement that his action was brought against certain named giant corporations. The court—so the story goes—told the prosecutor to proceed to his "next" point.

Eventually, of course, these three issues of "purpose," "effect," and "who," together with all other relevant facts in the particular litigation, are duly explored and weighed on the judicial scale. The court then returns to the controlling statutory provisions, to such past judicial rulings as seem relevant, and to the underlying congressional reasons. The pertinent words and purposes of Congress and the precedents and principles of the courts are thereupon placed with the facts into the judicial melting pot, and from these diverse ingredients the court eventually produces "a more or less concrete delineation of the standards that should be met in seeking a just decision upon the complicated facts of this case."[12]

It should be apparent, from this description of the antitrust laws in action, that the case-by-case decisions of the courts, in applying in litigated cases the concepts of Congress to the conduct of competitors, necessarily vary much as the prescriptions of doctors vary from patient to patient. In this field of law, no blind Justice mechanically applies to a businessman the rulings previously made in other cases. Instead our judiciary removes its blindfold in order both to see and to hear each defendant before deciding what, if any, judgment should be entered against him. Nevertheless, the general pattern of the antitrust decisions handed down to date—whose application to any specific company can best be determined by its counsel—would seem to conform to the rules of thumb discussed below.

Competitor Relationships

The application of the antitrust laws to the so-called horizontal relationships of a corporation with its competitors may be roughly summarized as follows:

First: A corporation may meet with its competitors. A businessman is not required to erect an iron barrier between himself and his com-

---

[11] White Motor Co. v. United States, 372 U.S. 253 (1963).
[12] United States v. Aluminum Company of America, 91 F. Supp. 333, 340 (S.D.N.Y. 1950).

petitors. He may join trade associations in which members of his industry meet, statistics on past transactions are compiled,[13] and procedures for detecting antisocial practices, such as fraud, are established.[14] With certain qualifications he may likewise participate in industry programs[15] and utilize common facilities[16] organized by his competitors to promote the best interests of his industry, where access to these joint projects is reasonably available to all members of the industry.[17]

Impersonal competitors, moreover, need not be personal enemies. An executive is free to maintain cordial individual relationships with his commercial adversaries, so long as his social visits do not embrace anticompetitive subjects[18] and his communications do not disclose secrets ordinarily withheld from commercial rivals.[19] As aptly summarized in a famous ruling: "A friendly relationship within . . . a long established industry is, in itself, not only natural but commendable and beneficial, as long as it does not breed illegal activities."[20]

Second: A corporation should not control its competitors. Our antitrust laws, nevertheless, obviously intervene in these relations of a businessman with his competitors when he seeks—not merely to be friends with these competitors—but to dominate them. His corporation is permitted, and even encouraged, to grow at the expense of its competitors, as, for example, by offering to its customers a better product or service at a lower cost than is available to them from those competitors.[21] But the larger the corporation the more carefully it must be scrutinized by the courts to see that its lawful commercial practices do not become, in its hands, by virtue of its size and power, lethal trade weapons for the elimination of its commercial rivals in violation of these laws on trade regulations.

The political faith of Congress in the wisdom of maintaining the independence of individual competitors, as well as its economic and moral belief in the desirability of free and open competition among these competitors, has led the courts to rule that no corporation consciously should seek or exercise the power to control the prices in, or to

---

[13] Maple Flooring Manufacturers Ass'n v. United States, 268 U.S. 563 (1925).
[14] Cement Manufacturers Protective Association v. United States, 268 U.S. 588 (1925).
[15] Eastern Railroad Presidents Conference v. Noerr Motor Freight, Inc., 365 U.S. 127 (1961); cf. California Motor Transport Co. v. Trucking Unlimited, 404 U.S. 508 (1972).
[16] United States v. Terminal Railroad Association of St. Louis, 224 U.S. 383 (1912).
[17] Associated Press v. United States, 326 U.S. 1 (1945).
[18] United States v. United States Steel Corporation, 251 U.S. 417, 440 (1920).
[19] United States v. American Linseed Oil Company, 262 U.S. 371 (1923).
[20] American Tobacco Co. v. United States, 328 U.S. 781, 793 (1946).
[21] Federal Trade Commission v. Curtis Publishing Company, 260 U.S. 568 (1923).

exclude others from, a market.[22] This means, of course, that a dominant company must not engage in any obvious monopolistic restraint, such as in cutting off rivals from essential sources of supply[23] or outlets,[24] or in coercing customers into ceasing to deal with those business adversaries (by refusing to trade with customers if they do).[25] But this also means that a dominant corporation may not utilize less obnoxious practices, such as the normally lawful use of leases of equipment[26] and of reciprocal licenses,[27] and even of its lawfully acquired facilities,[28] where the purpose or effect of these actions in the hands of such a powerful corporation is found to be complete regimentation of the market.

The large corporation, in other words, may be barred by the courts from using competitive weapons which remain available to the small. Where the drive and skill of the exceptional commercial golfer is too pronounced, he may in effect be given a competitive handicap. Otherwise his commercial opponents may too readily be discouraged and therefore default in the business tournament.

Third: A corporation should not conspire with its competitors. Our antitrust laws likewise intervene in the relations of a businessman with his competitors when he goes beyond normal community contacts and ventures into unnaturally close collaboration with those rivals. Because of the underlying belief of Congress in the virtues of competition, the laws seek to require the businessman who has elected to participate in our free economy to profit through competition and not by conspiracy. Accordingly, in applying the statutory language, the courts will strike down any arrangements between competitors—not authorized by Congress through regulatory legislation—whose purpose or effect is shown to be a substantial restraint of trade inconsistent with the competitive objective of these laws. Thus, the courts have repeatedly held that competitors may not agree upon the prices at which they collectively will buy[29] or sell,[30] the territories in which they will do business,[31] or the persons with whom each will deal.[32]

---

[22] United States v. Grinnell Corp., 384 U.S. 563 (1966).
[23] United States v. Reading Company, 226 U.S. 324 (1912).
[24] Zenith Radio Corporation v. Hazeltine Research, Inc., 395 U.S. 100 (1969).
[25] Lorain Journal Co. v. United States, 342 U.S. 143 (1951).
[26] United States v. United Shoe Machinery Corp., 110 F. Supp. 295 (D.Mass. 1953), aff'd, 347 U.S. 521 (1954).
[27] Transparent-Wrap Machine Corp. v. Stokes & Smith Co., 329 U.S. 637 (1947).
[28] Otter Tail Power Co. v. United States, 410 U.S. 366 (1973).
[29] Mandeville Island Farms, Inc. v. American Crystal Sugar Co., 334 U.S. 219 (1948).
[30] United States v. Socony-Vacuum Oil Co., Inc., 310 U.S. 150 (1940).
[31] United States v. Sealy, Inc., 388 U.S. 350 (1967).
[32] Radovich v. National Football League, 352 U.S. 445 (1957).

The businessman, moreover, should not attempt to avoid these rulings by concealing such a formal agreement, or by resorting to a mere informal arrangement with the same anticompetitive effect, with his competitors. His actions will tend to reveal that which his words seek to conceal. For example, an unnatural uniformity of action between competitors,[33] such as their raising prices simultaneously in a depression,[34] may be viewed by the courts as evidencing an unlawful arrangement as clearly as any written agreement. Again, the records of a telephone company listing calls between the private homes of competitors immediately prior to a price increase, if unexplained, may be embarrassing. Uniformity of action[35] and unusual telephone calls do not, of course, prove the existence of a conspiracy, but such conduct blazes a trail that may be readily followed by the imaginative prosecutor to determine whether or not such a conspiracy ever existed.

The businessman, furthermore, should not assume that only an agreement to eliminate all competition in his industry would be unlawful. Arrangements between competitors to dispense with commercial rivalry solely in one section of an industry, or merely with respect to particular conduct therein, may also be vulnerable. Competitors are not permitted even to establish codes of ethics which are limtied to specific industry practices if unreasonable or unfair restraints result. Among the partial restraints of this nature that have been prohibited are agreements between competitors that price changes are to be published and discounts are to be standardized,[36] deviations therefrom will be revealed upon request,[37] substandard products are to be dropped,[38] fraudulent merchants are to be boycotted,[39] fair trade contracts are to be enforced,[40] and arbitration is to be required of customers.[41]

Fourth: A corporation should not unfairly compete with its competitors. Our antitrust laws further advise the businessman, whether large or small, to compete fairly with his competitors. He is not penalized if he uses his ingenuity to develop new products[42] and new

---

[33] Interstate Circuit, Inc. v. United States, 306 U.S. 208 (1939).
[34] American Tobacco Co. v. United States, 328 U.S. 781 (1946).
[35] Theatre Enterprises, Inc. v. Paramount Film Distributing Corp., 346 U.S. 537 (1954).
[36] Sugar Institute, Inc. v. United States, 297 U.S. 553 (1936).
[37] United States v. Container Corp. of America, 393 U.S. 333 (1969).
[38] United States v. United States Gypsum Co., 333 U.S. 364 (1948).
[39] Fashion Originators' Guild of America v. Federal Trade Commission, 312 U.S. 457 (1941).
[40] United States v. Frankfort Distilleries, Inc., 324 U.S. 293 (1945).
[41] United States v. First National Pictures, Inc., 282 U.S. 44 (1930).
[42] United States v. E. I. du Pont de Nemours & Company, 351 U.S. 377 (1956).

methods of distribution.[43] He must, however, avoid practices opposed to good morals, that is, practices characterized by deception, bad faith, fraud, or oppression.[44]

The economic belief of Congress in competition, we have seen, has led to the condemnation by the courts of ruthless monopolistic practices obviously aimed at competitors, such as predatory price or rate cuts,[45] malicious discrimination,[46] coercion,[47] and exclusionary contracts tying up the market.[48] It has also caused the courts to prohibit allied conduct, such as the use of patents and unique supplies to restrict the markets of licensed competitors,[49] to control business in other goods, services, and machines[50] to estop their challenge of the validity of licensed rights[51] or otherwise to block off and fence in competitors.[52]

The moral convictions of Congress with respect to the need for fair dealing, however, have also resulted in the prohibition by the courts of practices, harmful to the public, whose continuation in the long run would drive out of business the ethical competitor. Conduct thus condemned included the misrepresentation of products[53] and the use, as promotions, of gambling devices.[54] Businessmen should compete, but they should compete under rules that permit the moral merchandiser to survive in a fair contest with the amoral.

Customer Relationships

The application of the antitrust laws to what is termed the vertical relationships of a corporation, that is to say with its customers, has resulted in a comparable set of rules.

First: A corporation may select its customers. The businessman normally is privileged under the antitrust laws to select, and thereafter to

[43] United States v. Columbia Steel Co., 334 U.S. 495 (1948).
[44] Federal Trade Commission v. Gratz, 253 U.S. 421 (1920).
[45] United States v. National Dairy Prods. Corp., 372 U.S. 29 (1963); Thomsen v. Cayser, 243 U.S. 66 (1917).
[46] Utah Pie Co. v. Continental Baking Co., 386 U.S. 685 (1967) and Porto Rican American Tobacco Co. of Porto Rico v. American Tobacco Co., 30 F.2d 234 (2d Cir. 1929), *cert. denied*, 279 U.S. 858 (1929).
[47] United States v. Crescent Amusement Co., 323 U.S. 173 (1944).
[48] Federal Trade Commission v. Motion Picture Advertising Service Co., Inc., 344 U.S. 392 (1953).
[49] United States v. Glaxo Group Limited, 410 U.S. 52 (1973).
[50] United States v. Loew's, Inc., 371 U.S. 38 (1962); Brulotte v. Thys Co., 379 U.S. 29 (1964).
[51] Lear, Inc. v. Adkins, 395 U.S. 653 (1969).
[52] United States v. Singer Mfg. Co., 374 U.S. 174 (1963); Hartford-Empire Co. v. United States, 323 U.S. 386 (1945).
[53] Federal Trade Commission v. Winsted Hosiery Company, 258 U.S. 483 (1922).
[54] Federal Trade Commission v. R. F. Keppel & Bro., Inc., 291 U.S. 304 (1934).

contract with, his customers. His corporation, as a general rule, may deal with some and refuse to deal with others,[55] may assure those selected that they alone will receive specified commodities[56] or services,[57] and may drop those outlets deemed to be unsatisfactory.[58]

The contracts of his corporation, moreover, may impose binding requirements on its customers where these obligations are reasonably ancillary to the conduct of its business with those buyers.[59] Thus, the corporation may exact assurances that a customer will use its best efforts to promote the corporation's products in (but not solely in) specified territories,[60] maintain proper quality and health safeguards,[61] and avoid misrepresentations to the public.[62] In industries where special necessity may be shown therefor, even total requirements contracts and other contractual restraints may be permitted.[63]

One of the most restrictive of the antitrust laws takes pains to reassure business with respect to its selection of customers:

> that nothing herein contained shall prevent persons engaged in selling goods, wares, or merchandise in commerce from selecting their own customers in bona fide transactions and not in restraint of trade. . . . [64]

Second: A corporation should not dominate its customers. The antitrust laws step into the relationship of a corporation with its customers, nevertheless, when the power of the former is exercised with the purpose or effect of controlling the competitive decisions of the latter. The statutory language and its underlying political intent to preserve the freedom of the little, independent merchant have resulted in the judicial caution that a seller may not, by use of his command over a major source of supply, destroy the competitive rights of the small buyer.

It follows that a corporation is not permitted to dictate the competitive decisions of its customers by the use of either formal or

---

[55] United States v. Colgate & Company, 250 U.S. 300 (1919).

[56] United States v. Bausch & Lomb Optical Co., 321 U.S. 707 (1944).

[57] Lawlor v. National Screen Service Corp., 352 U.S. 992 (1957).

[58] Packard Motor Car Company v. Webster Motor Car Company, 243 F.2d 418 (D.C. Cir. 1957), *cert. denied*, 355 U.S. 822 (1957); and Hudson Sales Corp. v. Waldrip, 211 F.2d 268 (5th Cir. 1954), *cert. denied*, 348 U.S. 821 (1954).

[59] United States v. American Tobacco Company, 221 U.S. 106 (1911).

[60] United States v. Philco Corporation, CCH 1956 Trade Cases para. 68,409 (E.D.Pa. 1956).

[61] See International Salt Co., Inc. v United States, 332 U.S. 392 (1947).

[62] Federal Trade Commission v. Sinclair Refining Company, 261 U.S. 463 (1923).

[63] Tampa Electric Co. v. Nashville Coal Co., 365 U.S. 320 (1961); cf. White Motor Co. v. United States, 372 U.S. 253 (1963).

[64] Robinson-Patman Price Discrimination Act sec. 1, 49 Stat. 1526 (1936), 15 U.S.C.A. sec. 13 (1970).

informal contracts with these distributors. Thus, in the absence of lawful fair trade contracts,[65] a corporation may not fix even by a consignment agreement the resale prices of its distributors.[66] Again, it may not safely require its customers to refrain from selling outside of defined territories.[67] Likewise, it may not prohibit outlets representing a substantial share of the market from utilizing the commodities[68] or services[69] of qualified alternative sources of supply through requiring them to enter into unreasonable tying or requirements contracts.[70]

The businessman also is forbidden to control the competitive policies of his customers through an abuse of his right to refuse to deal with them. We have seen that a group of competitors may not collectively agree upon the terms on which they will or will not deal with their customers.[71] In addition, even an individual seller, in the absence of such an agreement, may not enter into what amounts to a combination with its cooperating customers, pursuant to which it declines to sell to any noncooperating customers who reject the seller's instructions with respect to their resale prices,[72] customers,[73] and sources of supply.[74] A company may freely suggest prices, practices, and policies to its customers; but it must take care to limit those communications with its customers solely to such friendly advice.

Third: A corporation should not unduly discriminate between its customers. The antitrust laws also apply to a corporation's relationships with its customers when the former discriminates between its purchasers, with adverse competitive effects. The language and underlying purposes of Congress are best served by ensuring that all customers, when and if selected by a seller, have an equal start in their competitive race. This equality is denied, however, when any outlet is handicapped by its being required, without due cause, to pay to a seller a higher price for merchandise than other competing customers pay. This equality is also frustrated when an outlet receives from the seller, in aid of the resale of the merchandise, services, and facilities proportionately inferior to those that such other customers receive.

---

[65] Hudson Distributors, Inc. v. Eli Lilly & Co., 377 U.S. 386 (1964).

[66] Simpson v. Union Oil Co., 377 U.S. 13 (1964).

[67] United States v. Arnold, Schwinn & Co., 388 U.S. 365 (1967).

[68] Federal Trade Commission v. Texaco, Inc., 393 U.S. 223 (1968); Federal Trade Commission v. Brown Shoe Co., 384 U.S. 316 (1966).

[69] Northern Pacific Railway Company v. United States, 356 U.S. 1 (1958).

[70] Fortner Enterprises, Inc. v. United States Steel Corp., 394 U.S. 495 (1969).

[71] Radiant Burners, Inc. v. Peoples Gas Light & Coke Co., 364 U.S. 656 (1961).

[72] Albrecht v. Herald Co., 390 U.S. 145 (1968); United States v. Parke, Davis & Co., 362 U.S. 29 (1960).

[73] United States v. General Motors Corp., 384 U.S. 127 (1966).

[74] Perma Life Mufflers, Inc. v. International Parts Corp., 392 U.S. 134 (1968).

The courts, accordingly, have held that a corporation may not sell a commodity to one customer at one price, and simultaneously sell the same commodity to a competing customer at a substantially lower price,[75] unless the lower discriminatory price is affirmatively justified (as, for example, by cost savings[76] or by the necessity for the seller to meet an equally low price of a competing seller).[77] Similarly, this seller may not deny to one of its distributors[78] or customers of distributors[79] access, on proportionately equal terms, to equivalent services and facilities furnished by the seller to a competing distributor or customer. In short, a corporation that elects to sell to a purchaser may not, without statutory permission, deny to the purchaser prices and services equivalent to those granted to competing purchasers.

A buyer who knowingly receives an unjustified lower price[80] or more favorable payments for services and facilities,[81] it should be noted, may also violate the law. The purchasing power of a large buyer may legitimately be used to counterbalance the strength of a large seller,[82] but it may not be used with impunity to obtain a decisive unearned advantage over weaker purchasers.[83] Nor may a buyer justify an otherwise unlawful price discrimination by incorporating a purchasing subsidiary[84] or by fraudulently claiming that this discriminatory price is needed to meet a nonexistent lower competitive price.[85]

Fourth: A corporation should not deceive its customers. The antitrust laws are further involved in the relationships of a corporation with its customers when the former engages in unethical practices in its interstate dealings with its outlets. In this area of activity also, a businessman must avoid certain conduct opposed to the moral standards of the business community.[86]

---

[75] Federal Trade Commission v. Morton Salt Co., 334 U.S. 37 (1948). See also certain cases where the customers are not competing, for example, Utah Pie Co. v. Continental Baking Co., 386 U.S. 685 (1967).
[76] Federal Trade Commission, Advisory Committee on Cost Justification, *Report to the Federal Trade Commission* (1956).
[77] Standard Oil Co. v. Federal Trade Commission, 340 U.S. 231 (1951).
[78] Federal Trade Commission v. Simplicity Pattern Co., Inc., 360 U.S. 55 (1959).
[79] Federal Trade Commission v. Fred Meyer, Inc., 390 U.S. 341 (1968); Federal Trade Commission, *Guides for Advertising Allowances and Other Merchandising Payments and Services,* 4 CCH Trade Reg. Rep. para. 39,035 (1972).
[80] American Motor Specialties Co. v. Federal Trade Commission, 278 F.2d 225 (2d Cir. 1960).
[81] R. H. Macy & Co. v. Federal Trade Commission, 326 F.2d 445 (2d Cir. 1964).
[82] Automatic Canteen Company of America v. Federal Trade Commission, 346 U.S. 61 (1953).
[83] United States v. Griffith, 334 U.S. 100 (1948).
[84] Perkins v. Standard Oil Company of California, 393 U.S. 1013 (1969).
[85] Kroger Co. v. FTC, 438 F.2d 1372 (6th Cir.), *cert. denied,* 404 U.S. 871 (1971).
[86] Federal Trade Commission v. Gratz, 253 U.S. 421 (1920).

The ethical principles underlying the statutory prohibition of unfair and deceptive acts and practices, for example, have led to the condemnation of the commercial use of confusing names for products,[87] fictitious pricing,[88] deceptive descriptions of guarantees,[89] and "bait" advertising.[90] A businessman may neither conceal from the uninformed, nor mislead the gullible, in describing the nature, merits, and origin of his products and services in interstate and foreign[91] commerce.[92] In addition, he is required to substantiate the claims that he makes in his advertising and—to an uncertain degree—affirmatively to disclose other material facts which a consumer should know in order to be able to make an informed purchase.[93]

It should be noted that these ethical principles reach out to proscribe such practices whether or not competing sellers or buyers are thereby injured. Congress has taken the position that healthy competition can survive only if the channels of trade are kept free of contaminating contact with the unethical,[94] for the protection of society.[95]

Corporate Relationships

The application of the antitrust laws to the internal corporate relationships of a business organization is not as clearly defined, in the decisions handed down to date, as is the impact of these laws upon the relationships just discussed. The corporate rules currently evolving, however, would seem to be approximately as follows:

First: A corporation may manage its corporate family. It follows from the preceding discussion that our antitrust laws do not discourage a businessman in the extension of his old business or in the creation of a new business. The fact that, in this creative process, his business achieves success by reason of superior skill, superior products, natural advantages, or patents does not result in any violation of these laws.[96]

---

[87] Federal Trade Commission v. Algoma Lumber Co., 291 U.S. 67 (1934).
[88] Federal Trade Commission, *Guides Against Deceptive Pricing and Use of Word "Free,"* 14 CCH Trade Reg. Rep. paras. 39,015, 39,036 (8 January 1964 and 16 December 1972).
[89] Federal Trade Commission, *Guides Against Deceptive Advertising of Guarantees,* 4 CCH Trade Reg. Rep. para. 39,013 (adopted 26 April 1960).
[90] Federal Trade Commission, *Guides Against Bait Advertising,* 4 CCH Trade Reg. Rep. para. 39,011 (adopted 24 November 1959).
[91] Branch v. Federal Trade Commission, 141 F.2d 31 (7th Cir. 1944).
[92] Federal Trade Commission v. Colgate-Palmolive Co., 380 U.S. 374 (1965).
[93] Firestone Tire & Rubber Co. v. FTC, 481 F.2d 246 (6th Cir.), *cert. denied,* 414 U.S. 1112 (1973).
[94] Federal Trade Commission v. R. F. Keppel & Bro., Inc., 291 U.S. 304 (1934).
[95] Federal Trade Commission v. Sperry & Hutchinson Co., 405 U.S. 233 (1972).
[96] United States v. United Shoe Machinery Corp., 110 F. Supp. 295 (D. Mass. 1953), *aff'd,* 347 U.S. 521 (1954).

The antitrust laws, moreover, in no way restrict the businessman in incorporating and thereafter in making the competitive decisions for any such extended or new business. He may not safely represent, contrary to fact, that any such subsidiary is independent of another subsidiary.[97] Similarly, he may not buy a minority interest in a major competitor and claim the right to operate it as a subsidiary.[98] However, where he creates the business of a subsidiary and openly acknowledges it to be an incorporated division of the parent, he should be permitted to fix its prices,[99] control its markets,[100] and direct its purchases.[101]

The statutory section most critical of stock acquisitions carefully makes the following provision:

> Nor shall anything herein contained prevent a corporation engaged in commerce from causing the formation of subsidiary corporations for the actual carrying on of their immediate lawful business, or the natural and legitimate branches or extentions thereof, or from owning and holding all or part of the stock of such subsidiary corporations, when the effect of such formation is not to substantially lessen competition.[102]

Second: A corporation should not monopolize the markets of its corporate family. The language and intent of the antitrust laws nevertheless frown upon the malicious use by a substantial corporation of its subsidiaries or divisions to destroy its competitors.

In the past, the economic benefits of free competition were denied to our economy by the old trusts and combinations which sought to impose their wills upon their competitors. Accordingly, the old Cash Register,[103] Corn Products,[104] DuPont,[105] Eastman,[106] Harvester,[107] Standard Oil,[108] and American Tobacco[109] aggregations were dis-

---

[97] Kiefer-Stewart Co. v. Joseph E. Seagram & Sons, Inc., 340 U.S. 211 (1951).
[98] Timken Roller Bearing Co. v. United States, 341 U.S. 593 (1951).
[99] United States v. Arkansas Fuel Oil Corp., CCH 1960 Trade Cases para. 69,619 (N.D.Okla. 1960).
[100] Sunkist Growers, Inc. v. Winckler & Smith Citrus Prods. Co., 370 U.S. 19 (1962).
[101] United States v. Columbia Steel Co., 334 U.S. 495 (1948).
[102] Clayton Act sec. 7, 38 Stat. 731 (1914), *as amended,* 15 U.S.C.A. sec. 18 (1970).
[103] Patterson v. United States, 222 Fed. 599 (6th Cir. 1915), *cert. denied,* 238 U.S. 635 (1915).
[104] United States v. Corn Products Refining Co., 234 Fed. 964 (S.D.N.Y 1916), *appeal dismissed,* 249 U.S. 621 (1919).
[105] United States v. E. I. du Pont de Nemours & Company, 188 Fed. 127 (C.C.D.Del. 1911).
[106] United States v. Eastman Kodak Co., 226 Fed. 62 (W.D.N.Y. 1915), *final decree entered,* 230 Fed. 522 (W.D.N.Y. 1916), *appeal dismissed,* 255 U.S. 578 (1921).
[107] United States v. International Harvester Co., 214 Fed. 987 (D.Minn. 1914).
[108] Standard Oil Company of New Jersey v. United States, 221 U.S. 1 (1911).
[109] United States v. American Tobacco Company, 221 U.S. 106 (1911).

solved when they sought to control their respective industries. In more recent days the modern corporation has sought, through more subtle uses of its subsidiaries or divisions, to achieve comparable results adverse to a competitive economy. This more sophisticated method of monopoly, however, has likewise been condemned. Thus the courts have held that one branch of a company may not use its monopolistic control over the supply of products,[110] or its dominance in a local market for those products,[111] to deny these products to independent competitors of a branch of this company in another market. Similarly, they have held that a dominant producer may not transfer a commodity to its captive fabricating division at a substantially lower cost than the price at which it sells to independent fabricators.[112]

As noted in the previous discussion of competitor relationships, the monopolization of a line of commerce, even through the use of otherwise lawful practices such as leasing, has been condemned. In short, the intentional acquisition or enjoyment of the power of economic life or death over others in our economy, where not justified by superior industrial skills or advantages thrust upon a business organization, is prohibited.

Third: A corporation should not misuse the muscle of its corporate family. There are increasing signs, moreover, that the use by any substantial corporation of the strength of one division merely to give an unfair competitive advantage to another of its divisions will raise substantial antitrust problems. For example, the threat by a parent to compete with its customers through a subsidiary or division, unless these customers purchase exclusively from or sell out to the parent, is a debatable practice in industry.[113] Again, the employment of reciprocity, by which the purchasing power of one corporate unit is used to require sellers to purchase in return from another unit of the corporation, gives to the integrated enterprise an alien competitive weapon not available to its nonintegrated competitors.[114] Similarly the use of the facilities[115] or profits of a parent[116] or one line of its products[117] to give a decisive competitive advantage to another branch of that corpo-

---

[110] United States v. Paramount Pictures, Inc., 334 U.S. 131 (1948).
[111] United States v. Griffith, 334 U.S. 100 (1948).
[112] United States v. Aluminum Company of America, 148 F.2d 416 (2d Cir. 1945).
[113] Poller v. Columbia Broadcasting System, Inc., 368 U.S. 464 (1962); Federal Trade Commission v. Eastman Kodak Company, 274 U.S. 619 (1927).
[114] Federal Trade Commission v. Consolidated Foods Corp., 380 U.S. 592 (1965).
[115] Otter Tail Power Co. v. United States, 410 U.S. 366 (1973).
[116] United States v. New York Great Atlantic & Pacific Tea Co., 173 F.2d 79 (7th Cir. 1949).
[117] United States v. United Shoe Machinery Corp., 110 F. Supp. 295 (D.Mass. 1953), aff'd, 347 U.S. 521 (1954).

rate family may result in the unfair competition by this integrated branch with its competitors.

The most controversial area in which the competitive use of superior resources is being scrutinized is the practice of below cost selling. The predatory employment of such pricing has been held to be a criminal offense, and its discriminatory use has been viewed under some circumstances to be a civil violation.[118]

Whether and to what extent in particular instances such intracorporate transactions of an integrated company will be condemned as unfair to the nonintegrated independent competitor cannot be accurately forecast. Presumably much will depend upon the purpose, the effect, and the participants involved. The business executive who launches an offensive attack upon a small competitor of one division with the collective strength of all units of his corporation, however, would be well advised to weigh the increasing distaste of our courts for "the utilization of economic power in one market to curtail competition in another."[119]

Fourth: A corporation should not indiscriminately multiply, through mergers with others, its corporate family. The antitrust laws, furthermore, generally oppose the expansion of a substantial corporation through its acquisition of the stock or assets of a competing unit or division of another substantial company. The political objective of preserving the market structure of vigorously competing buyers and sellers would be frustrated if the horizontal merger of such competitors were freely sanctioned. Accordingly, the merger by a large, aggressive company with a solvent substantial competitor has been condemned out of hand.[120] A series of such acquisitions of competitors by a substantial corporation has also been held to be unlawful.[121] Even a large company competing in the sale of alternative forms of a product,[122] or representing a merely potential source of the same product,[123] has been barred from merging its business with a substantial existing producer of that product.

All mergers of competitors, of course, are not prohibited. Thus, small competitors may be permitted to bind themselves together in

---

[118] United States v. National Dairy Prods. Corp., 372 U.S. 29 (1963); and Utah Pie Co. v. Continental Baking Co., 386 U.S. 685 (1967).
[119] Atlantic Refining Co. v. Federal Trade Commission, 381 U.S. 357, 369 (1965).
[120] United States v. Von's Grocery Co., 384 U.S. 270 (1966); United States v. Pabst Brewing Co., 384 U.S. 546 (1966).
[121] United States v. Jerrold Electronics Corporation, 187 F. Supp. 545 (E.D. Pa. 1960), aff'd, 365 U.S. 567 (1961).
[122] United States v. Continental Can Co., 378 U.S. 441 (1964).
[123] Jos. Schlitz Brewing Co. v. United States, 385 U.S. 37 (1966); United States v. El Paso Natural Gas Co., 376 U.S. 651 (1964).

order to provide a sufficiently large economic raft on which to ride out a competitive storm.[124]   Also, both large and small may acquire a competitive business where either (a) it is of little competitive significance[125] or (b) it is a failing company[126] for which there is no alternative purchaser (whose acquisition may represent less of a competitive threat).[127]   Nevertheless, it seems clear that the eye of the antitrust needle has appreciably narrowed for the acquisitions by substantial corporations of other viable businesses which offer either vigorous or potentially effective sources of competition.[128]

The antitrust laws, moreover, would appear increasingly to raise doubts with respect to the legality of the expansion of a corporation through its acquisition of the stock or assets of other substantial companies, whether or not they are competitors. Judicial decisions and enforcement actions during past years reflect a growing tendency to question substantial mergers and acquisitions involving large companies particularly where a major supplier or customer of the acquiring company is involved.[129]   Thus the acquisition by a large supplier of over 20 percent of the stock of a customer representing a substantial share of its consumer market has been prohibited.[130] Similarly, a series of major mergers which has integrated a seller with its customers has been proscribed.[131] Indeed a dominant corporation must even debate whether or not to acquire other corporations which are neither competitors, suppliers, nor customers, where the probable effect thereof may be substantially to increase its competitive strength.[132]

Doubt has also been thrown upon the legality of the joint acquisition by two competitors of the stock of a third company organized by the former two corporations. The creation of such a joint venture is not per se unlawful.[133] In fact, such joint undertakings often are essential to the development of new technology and the entrance into new markets.[134] A corporation which is capable of undertaking with-

---

[124] H.R. Rep. No. 1191, 81st Cong., 1st sess. (1949); cf. United States v. Republic Steel Corporation, 11 F. Supp. 117 (N.D. Ohio 1935).
[125] United States v. General Dynamics Corp., 415 U.S. 486 (1974); cf. United States v. Connecticut National Bank, 418 U.S. 656 (1974).
[126] International Shoe Company v. Federal Trade Commission, 280 U.S. 291 (1930).
[127] Citizen Publishing Co. v. United States, 394 U.S. 131 (1969); also United States v. Greater Buffalo Press, Inc., 402 U.S. 549 (1971).
[128] United States v. Falstaff Brewing Corporation, 410 U.S. 526 (1973) and CCH 1974–2 Trade Cases para. 75, 315 (D.R.I. 1974); see United States v. Marine Bancorporation, Inc., 418 U.S. 602 (1974).
[129] Ford Motor Co. v. United States, 405 U.S. 562 (1972).
[130] United States v. E. I. du Pont de Nemours & Company, 353 U.S. 586 (1957).
[131] Brown Shoe Co. v. United States, 370 U.S. 294 (1962).
[132] Federal Trade Commission v. Consolidated Foods Corp., 380 U.S. 592 (1965); Federal Trade Commission v. Proctor & Gamble Co., 386 U.S. 568 (1967).
[133] United States v. Imperial Chem. Indus., Ltd., 105 F. Supp. 215, 244 (S.D.N.Y. 1952).
[134] United States v. E. I. du Pont de Nemours & Company, 351 U.S. 377 (1956).

out assistance the function of such a joint venture, however, should at least be cautious in sharing that venture with a potential competitor.[135]

Mergers and joint ventures as yet are not, and should not be, condemned merely because they involve large companies. The merger-minded executive dreaming today of expanding his corporate borders through acquisitions, nevertheless, should keep in mind that at best his form of growth must run the gauntlet of critical scrutiny from the Department of Justice[136] and the Federal Trade Commission[137] and, at worst, could be condemned if it threatens to restrain competition even in a small community.[138] Indeed, it is the view of some judicial Canutes that the courts must stop the current wave of mergers, regardless of the business reasons which may be advanced for an individual acquisition. For the courts have stressed that

> [w]e cannot fail to recognize Congress' desire to promote competition through the protection of viable, small, locally owned businesses. Congress appreciated that occasional higher costs and prices might result from the maintenance of fragmented industries and markets. It resolved these competing considerations in favor of decentralization.[139]

---

[135]United States v. Penn-Olin Chem. Co., 378 U.S. 158 (1964).
[136] Department of Justice, *Merger Guidelines*, 1 CCH Trade Reg. Rep. para. 4510.
[137] Federal Trade Commission, *Merger Notification Program*, 1 CCH Trade Reg. Rep. para. 4540.
[138] United States v. Phillipsburg National Bank and Trust Company, 399 U.S. 350 (1970).
[139] Brown Shoe Co. v. United States, 370 U.S. 294, 344 (1962).

5

THE ENFORCEMENT OF
THE ANTITRUST LAWS

Flexible Administration

It should interest the lay reader to consider now the enforcement provisions of the antitrust laws and to discover how, to a striking degree, they parallel the flexible approach of the substantive provisions of these laws. For this legislation in similar fashion makes general provision for action by alternative agencies to effectuate the competitive objective of the antitrust laws, and it authorizes these agencies to exercise substantial discretion in the use of the enforcement powers thereby delegated to them.

Congress has generally sought, through the procedural provisions of the antitrust laws, to provide for alternative agencies with cumulative remedies to enforce these laws. Thus, initially Congress has empowered the Department of Justice, as public prosecutor, to bring civil and criminal actions.[1] Next, it has authorized the Federal Trade Commission, through administrative procedures, to encourage voluntary compliance and to compel involuntary compliance.[2] Finally, it has provided for miscellaneous sanctions at the hands of other regulatory agencies,[3] and for injunctive relief and treble damages in the course of private actions brought by injured persons.[4]

These procedural provisions of the antitrust laws collectively ensure the policing of industry, much as their substantive prohibitions comprehensively cover all undesirable restraints. For example, the Department of Justice and private parties are empowered to move

---

[1] Sherman Antitrust Act, 26 Stat. 209 (1890), *as amended,* 15 U.S.C.A. secs. 1–8 (Supp. I 1975), and Clayton Act, 38 Stat. 730 (1914), *as amended,* 15 U.S.C.A. secs. 12–27 (1970).
[2] Federal Trade Commission Act, 38 Stat. 717 (1914), *as amended,* 15 U.S.C.A. secs. 41–58 (Supp. I 1975), and Clayton Act (see note 1 above).
[3] See, for example, Clayton Act sec. 11, 38 Stat. 734 (1914); 15 U.S.C.A. sec. 21 (1970).
[4] Sherman Antitrust and Clayton Acts (see note 1 above).

against the present and probable restraints, respectively, of the Sherman and Clayton (as amended by the Robinson-Patman) Acts. Again, the Federal Trade Commission is authorized to act against the probable and unfair restraints of the Clayton (plus Robinson-Patman) and Federal Trade Commission Acts. Like the famous text in Galatians, these statutory remedies entail multiple damnations of forbidden restraints, one punishment sure if another fails.

The employment of private persons as public policemen in the enforcement of these laws, it should be noted, is intended to plug, with the self-interest of individual litigants, any gaps in the disinterested patrolling by the government agencies: "Congress intended to use private self interest as a means of enforcement and to arm injured persons with private means to retribution . . . ."[5]

Congress, through the procedural provisions of the antitrust laws, has also granted to these public and private agencies broad discretion in determining when and whom to sue in the enforcement of these laws, much in the manner in which it has delegated to the courts sweeping authority to exercise discretion in their interpretation of these laws. Thus, the department may bring, either alternatively or simultaneously, its civil and criminal actions.[6] Again, the commission may pursue both its voluntary and its involuntary procedures.[7] Likewise, the private plaintiff may sue either for injunctive relief, for damages, or both.[8] These enforcement agencies, moreover, need not defer to each other. In practice, the department and the commission avoid proceeding simultaneously against the same persons for the same offenses, by the use of a clearance procedure through which they check with each other before initiating their respective investigations. The law, however, does not require either to defer to the other.[9] In practice, likewise, private plaintiffs usually prefer to await successful government litigation before bringing suit, although the statute permits them to anticipate or parallel any government proceedings.

The grant in the statutes of wide discretion in particular to the government agencies, in their initiation of enforcement proceedings, has been expressly recognized by the courts: "Just as the Sherman Act itself permits the attorney general to bring simultaneous civil and criminal suits against a defendant based on the same misconduct, so the Sherman Act and the Trade Commission Act provide the Govern-

---

[5] Bruce's Juices, Inc. v American Can Co., 330 U.S. 743, 751 (1947).
[6] Standard Sanitary Manufacturing Company v. United States, 226 U.S. 20 (1912).
[7] Federal Trade Commission, *Procedures and Rules of Practice*, 16 C.F.R. ch. 1, subch. A; 3 CCH Trade Reg. Rep. para. 9801 et seq. (1974).
[8] Clayton Act, secs. 4, 16, 38 Stat. 731, 737 (1914); 15 U.S.C.A. secs. 15, 26 (1970).
[9] United States Alkali Export Ass'n v. United States, 325 U.S. 196 (1945).

ment with cumulative remedies against activity detrimental to com
petition."[10]

Department Proceedings

The Department of Justice, through its Antitrust Division, enforces
the laws within the scope of its jurisdiction primarily as a public
prosecutor seeking to compel compliance in adversary proceedings.
Although the department will render carefully guarded advisory opinions on prospective mergers and other contemplated transactions,[11] it
operates essentially as a litigator. As an arm of the executive branch of
the government, its enforcement policies reflect closely the current
views of the administration in power on antitrust policing.

The mechanics of the department's procedures are substantially
as follows: The department acts either upon the receipt of an external
communication from a private or public complainant who claims to
have been injured by a trade restraint or—increasingly—as the result
of some internal study. This matter is then assigned for evaluation to a
trial staff, located either in Washington or in a field office. If further
information appears to be necessary, successive resort to a prelimi-
nary review of the readily accessible industry and governmental information, to a more sweeping FBI investigation, to a civil investiga-
tive demand, and/or to a formal grand jury proceeding may result. The
grand jury, however, may be used only when criminal proceedings
are contemplated.[12]

Upon completion of this investigation, the department may decide that no further action should be taken. In this event, the file is
closed. On the other hand, the department may determine that a
proceeding should be instituted. In this case the department must
decide whether to institute a criminal proceeding, to bring a civil suit,
or both. The criminal action is brought to punish wrongdoing and is
penal in nature; whereas the civil action is instituted solely to forbid
future violations of the law.[13]

Should the Department of Justice eventually elect to bring a criminal proceeding, it may initiate such an action either by obtaining a
grand jury indictment or by filing a formal notice called an information. In such a proceeding, fines may be imposed on each corporate
and individual[14] defendant for each violation of a section of the Sherman Act. Such fines are not tax deductible and possibly may not be

---

[10] Federal Trade Commission v. Cement Institute, 333 U.S. 683, 694 (1948).
[11] See the department's *Business Review Procedure*, 2 Trade Reg. Rep. para. 8559.
[12] United States v. Proctor & Gamble Co., 356 U.S. 677 (1958).
[13] Hartford-Empire Co. v. United States, 323 U.S. 386 (1945); 324 U.S. 570 (1945).
[14] United States v. Wise, 370 U.S. 405 (1962).

reimbursable by the corporate employer. Additional consequences for individual defendants may include surrender to the custody of the U. S. marshall, fingerprinting, posting of bonds, sentencing, handcuffs, and a term in jail.[15] The cumulative nature of these criminal penalties in the past is illustrated by the *Safeway* proceeding in which a corporate defendant was fined a total of $105,000 and a principal executive was both fined $75,000 and placed on probation with two concurrent one-year jail sentences. Similarly, in the electrical companies case, the corporate defendants were fined a total of $1,787,000, their executives were fined an aggregate of $137,500, and seven of these executives received and served 30-day jail sentences.[16] In the future, by reason of a 1974 amendment of the Sherman Act, violation of this statute may result in a fine not to exceed $1 million if the defendant is a corporation, a fine not to exceed $100 thousand if the defendant is an individual person, and imprisonment for a term not to exceed three years in the case of such an individual person—plus attendant loss of civil rights.[17]

As remarked by Judge Knox in the *Carboloy* case:

> Undoubtedly the temper of the country has changed and the temper of the judiciary has changed over what it was twenty or twenty-five years ago, and I suppose that industry must adjust itself to such changes and those who are in executive positions in large businesses must realize the need to conform to present day mores. One of them I suppose is that in interstate commerce in a large industry, price-fixing is taboo, and those who engage in it run serious risk of being severely punished.[18]

Should the Department of Justice decide to bring a proceeding in equity, it initiates the action by serving and filing a civil complaint. This civil action may parallel a criminal action directed to the same violation,[19] and may be pursued even though the criminal action is decided adversely to the government.[20] Settlement of such an action through entry of a judgment by consent of the parties is permitted only if a public impact statement with respect to the settlement is filed by

[15] Gulf Coast Shrimpers and Oystermen's Association v. United States, 236 F.2d 658 (5th Cir. 1956), *cert. denied,* 352 U.S. 927 (1956); Las Vegas Merchant Plumbers Ass'n v. United States, 210 F.2d 732 (9th Cir. 1954), *cert. denied,* 348 U.S. 817, *rehearing denied,* 348 U.S. 889 (1954); United States v. McDonough Co., 180 F. Supp. 511 (S.D.Ohio 1959).
[16] United States v. Safeway Stores, Incorporated, 20 F.R.D. 451 (N.D.Tex. 1957); and Richard Austin Smith, "The Incredible Electrical Conspiracy," *Fortune,* vol. 63 (April 1961), pp. 132–37 and (May 1961), pp. 161–64.
[17] Sherman Antitrust Act secs. 1–2, 26 Stat. 209 (1890), *as amended,* 15 U.S.C.A. secs. 1–2 (Supp. I 1975).
[18] United States v. General Electric, Transcript of 12 November 1948, p. 2993.
[19] Standard Sanitary Manufacturing Company v. United States, 226 U.S. 20 (1912).
[20] United States v. National Association of Real Estate Boards, 339 U.S. 485 (1950).

thc department and the terms of the judgment are published sixty days in advance of its effective date. At the conclusion of such a civil action a defendant may find himself required to deal where he does not want to deal,[21] license where he does not wish to license,[22] surrender contractual and other rights,[23] and be subjected in perpetuity to government visitations.[24] The court injunction, moreover, may order the divestiture of stock[25] or of assets,[26] and even the outright dissolution of offending organizations.[27] Further relief may subsequently be ordered.[28]

In short, the department is not limited to requesting, in a civil proceeding, the mere cessation of past objectionable conduct: "When the purpose to restrain trade appears from a clear violation of law, it is not necessary that all of the untraveled roads to that end be left open and that only the worn one be closed."[29]

Commission Proceedings

The Federal Trade Commission, in enforcing the antitrust laws, seeks to supplement departmental litigation in the courts with less formal administrative procedures. Its role is to obtain antitrust compliance both through persuasion and through litigation. As a quasi-judicial body whose members are drawn from more than one political party, it is less apt than the department to modify its policies in sympathy with changing political views. It therefore attempts to enlist support, both within and without government, for its enforcement programs by stressing the "expertise" of its commissioners and staff.

Action by the commission, as in the case of the department, usually is the result of a complaint from industry or from some source in government. The instances in which it acts on its own initiative, however, have been more frequent than in the case of the department. Those matters deemed by it to merit careful scrutinizing are usually referred to one of the commission's Washington or regional offices for investigation. This office then utilizes the courtesy of informal requests and the coercion of formal demands to obtain the facts relevant to the issues raised. A report of the results of the investigation is eventually submitted to the commission. In the alter-

---

[21] Associated Press v. United States, 326 U.S. 1 (1945).
[22] Besser Manufacturing Co. v. United States, 343 U.S. 444 (1952).
[23] Northern Pacific Railway Company v. United States, 356 U.S. 1 (1958).
[24] United States v. Bausch & Lomb Optical Co., 321 U.S. 707 (1944).
[25] United States v. National Lead Co., 332 U.S. 319 (1947).
[26] Ford Motor Co. v. United States, 405 U.S. 562 (1972).
[27] International Boxing Club of New York, Inc. v. United States, 358 U.S. 242 (1959).
[28] United States v. United Shoe Machinery Corp., 391 U.S. 244 (1968).
[29] International Salt Co., Inc. v. United States, 332 U.S. 392, 400 (1947).

native, compulsory reports under section 6 of the Federal Trade Commission Act may be resorted to in order to secure the facts desired.

Should the commission then determine that action by it is required, it may then take one of two courses. On the one hand it may be content, in the exercise of its discretion, to request, from those it has investigated, a voluntary undertaking to comply with the law. On the other hand, it may decide to seek a formal commission order requiring involuntary conformance to the law.

In the exercise of its discretionary powers to encourage voluntary compliance, the commission may dispose of matters under investigation informally, by what is known as adminstrative treatment, where the issues raised are of relatively minor public interest. These techniques in effect close the file after receipt from the person or persons investigated of satisfactory assurances of future conformance to the standards laid down by the commission's staff with respect to the matters investigated. In addition, in order to assist informed law observance, the commission may give confidential advice to individual applicants,[30] and may publish explanatory guides[31] and rules[32] for the information of all industry setting forth its views on the application of the law to basic industrial problems.

Congress has now expressly authorized the commission to expand the use of its guides and rules (following public notice and other procedural safeguards) in part, as follows:

> Section 18. (a) (1) The commission may prescribe—
>
> (A) interpretive rules and general statements of policy with respect to unfair or deceptive acts or practices in or affecting commerce [within the meaning of section 5 (a) (1) of this Act], and
>
> (B) rules which define with specificity acts or practices which are unfair or deceptive acts or practices in or affecting commerce (within the meaning of such section 5 (a) (1). Rules under this subparagraph may include requirements prescribed for the purpose of preventing such acts or practices.
>
> . . .
>
> (d) (3) When any rule under subsection (a) (1) (B) takes effect a subsequent violation thereof shall constitute an unfair or deceptive act or practice in violation of section 5

---

[30] Federal Trade Commission, *Procedures and Rules of Practice,* 16 C.F.R. secs. 1.1–1.4, 3 CCH Trade Reg. Rep. paras. 9801.1–9801.4 (1974).

[31] See, for example, Federal Trade Commission, *Guides Against Deceptive Pricing,* 4 CCH Trade Reg. Rep. para. 39,015 (1964); and *Guides for Advertising Allowances and Other Merchandising Payments and Services,* 4 CCH Trade Reg. Rep. para. 39,035 (1972).

[32] Federal Trade Commission, *Procedures and Rules of Practice,* 16 C.F.R. secs. 1.11–1.16, 3 CCH Trade Reg. Rep. paras. 9801.11–9801.16 (1974).

(a) (1) of this Act, unless the commission otherwise expressly provides in such rule.[33] [ATRR No. 694, 24 December 1974, at F-4]

In the exercise of its alternative powers to require involuntary compliance, the commission issues a complaint when, in its opinion, the public interest so requires.[34] The matter is then heard before, and is decided by, an administrative law judge from whose initial decision and orders an appeal to the commission may be sought. In turn, the commission's decision and order may be appealed to the courts. The commission has a wide discretion in its choice of provisions for inclusion in these orders. For example, it may enjoin not only the specific unlawful action taken, but alternative methods of achieving the same result as well.[35] Violations of its orders and rules regarding unfair or deceptive practices by a person subject thereto may result in fines of $10 thousand per offense or $10 thousand per day for each day of a continuing offense.[36] In addition, knowing violations by any other person of such of its orders or rules as proscribe an unfair or deceptive act or practice may similarly be punished by these fines of $10 thousand. Furthermore, "consumer redress" actions may be instituted in the courts by the commission under certain circumstances to obtain rescission or reformation of contracts, refund of money or return of property, and/or payment of damages for unfair or deceptive acts or practices in violation of such orders or rules.[37] In short, "The Commission has wide discretion in its choice of a remedy deemed adequate to cope with the unlawful practices in this area of trade and commerce."[38]

Private Proceedings

A private person also is authorized to proceed under the antitrust laws by (1) suing for three-fold the damages inflicted upon his business or property by an antitrust violator; (2) petitioning for injunctive relief against that wrongdoer; and/or (3) raising as a defense, in actions brought against him, the antitrust violations of the plaintiff. Such a private prosecutor has been increasingly successful in the courts, with the result that the threat of his private litigation is at times more effective than the threat of government action in deterring the preda-

---

[33] Federal Trade Commission Act sec. 18, 15 U.S.C.A. sec. 57(a) (Supp. I 1975).
[34] Federal Trade Commission v. Klesner, 280 U.S. 19 (1929).
[35] Federal Trade Commission v. National Lead Co., 352 U.S. 419 (1957).
[36] Federal Trade Commission Act, 38 Stat. 717 (1914), as amended, 15 U.S.C.A. secs. 41–58 (Supp. I 1975); also United States v. ITT Continental Baking Co., 95 S. Ct. 926 (1975).
[37] Federal Trade Commission Act sec. 19, 15 U.S.C.A. sec. 57 (b) (Supp. I 1975).
[38] Jacob Siegel Co. v. Federal Trade Commission, 327 U.S. 608, 611 (1946).

tory businessman from seeking a quick profit at the expense of a vulnerable competitor or customer.

The right of a private person to sue for treble damages and for equitable relief where he is the victim of antitrust violation is expressly provided by statute.[39] Among those who have been held entitled to sue for damages and/or injunctive relief have been competitors,[40] customers,[41] licensees,[42] suppliers,[43] and apparently even football players[44] and minority stockholders.[45] This right of a private person to sue for relief under the antitrust law, moreover, is made more effective by a statutory provision to the effect that a final judgment entered in a contested Department of Justice action may be used in the subsequent private action to establish, in the absence of convincing proof to the contrary, that the antitrust laws had been violated.[46] A further statutory provision suspends the statute of limitations applicable to his private action during the pendency of a parallel department—and even of a commission—proceeding.[47] Class actions brought on behalf of allegedly injured private parties are also authorized.[48]

The damages awarded to a plaintiff in a treble damage action have, on occasion, been very liberal on the theory that "a defendant whose wrongful conduct has rendered difficult the ascertainment of the precise damages suffered by the plaintiff, is not entitled to complain that they cannot be measured with the same exactness and precision as would otherwise be possible."[49]

The right of a private person to defeat actions brought against him as a defendant, by raising the defense of antitrust violation on the part of the plaintiff, is not set forth expressly by statute. Nevertheless, one who is sued on the basis of a contract intrinsically unlawful under the antitrust laws,[50] or upon patents then being affirmatively misused in

---

[39] See Clayton Act secs. 4, 16, 38 Stat. 731, 737 (1914); 15 U.S.C.A. secs. 15, 26 (1970).
[40] Continental Ore Co. v. Union Carbide and Carbon Corp., 370 U.S. 690 (1962).
[41] Kiefer-Stewart Co. v. Joseph E. Seagram & Sons, Inc., 340 U.S. 211 (1951).
[42] Bigelow v. RKO Radio Pictures, Inc., 327 U.S. 251 (1946).
[43] Mandeville Island Farms, Inc. v. American Crystal Sugar Co., 334 U.S. 219 (1948).
[44] Radovich v. National Football League, 352 U.S. 445 (1957).
[45] Fanchon & Marco, Inc. v. Paramount Pictures, Inc., 202 F.2d 731 (2d Cir.), *cert. denied,* 345 U.S. 964 (1953).
[46] Emich Motors Corp. v. General Motors Corp., 340 U.S. 558 (1951).
[47] Minnesota Mining and Manufacturing Co. v. New Jersey Wood Finishing Co., 381 U.S. 311 (1965).
[48] American Pipe & Construction Co. v. Utah, 414 U.S. 538 (1974); see State of Hawaii v. Standard Oil of California, 405 U.S. 251 (1972).
[49] Eastman Kodak Co. of New York v. Southern Photo Materials Co., 273 U.S. 359, 379 (1927).
[50] Compare Continental Wall Paper Company v. Louis Voight & Sons Company, 212 U.S. 227 (1909), with Connolly v. Union Sewer Pipe Company, 184 U.S. 540 (1902), and Bruce's Juices, Inc. v. American Can Co., 330 U.S. 743 (1947).

violation of those laws,[51] has been permitted not only to defeat recovery but to counterclaim for treble damages.[52] For example, a suit brought to enforce a contract or sale,[53] or a patent license agreement,[54] has been barred where the defendant has been able to establish an antitrust violation on the part of the plaintiff inherent in the causes of action being asserted. A private person may also have comparable antitrust defenses in a trademark action brought against him.[55]

The paradox of a defendant charged with contractual or other wrongdoing thus being able to defeat an otherwise proper recovery because of the antitrust sins of the plaintiff, however, is being scrutinized more carefully by the courts.[56] While a private person is encouraged to advance antitrust compliance by means of individual or class actions which challenge antitrust violations on the part of other parties,[57] he is increasingly discouraged from raising such violations as a defense to excuse his failure to perform his own purely private obligations. The Supreme Court has significantly pointed out, "As a defense to an action based on contract, the plea of illegality based on violation of the Sherman Act has not met with much favor in this court."[58]

The collective remedies of public and private plaintiffs under the antitrust laws are more than adequate without any necessity for broadening these antitrust defenses of a defaulting defendant. Congress has been forced to be general in phrasing its substantive antitrust prohibitions, but—as seen above—it has been more than specific in enumerating the many procedural punishments for those who violate these prohibitions. Individual[59] as well as corporate antitrust defendants are being subjected to increasingly severe punishment for debatable infractions of the antitrust laws, without being permitted to plead in mitigation either the ambiguity of the applicable law[60] or the equally grave offenses of other litigants[61] and nonlitigants.[62] Why, therefore, should other defendants be forgiven their deliberate de-

---

[51] Morton Salt Co. v. G. S. Suppiger Co., 314 U.S. 488 (1942).

[52] Zenith Radio Corp. v. Hazeltine Research, Inc., 401 U.S. 321 (1971).

[53] Continental Wall Paper Company v. Louis Voight & Sons Company, 212 U.S. 227 (1909).

[54] Edward Katzinger Co. v. Chicago Metallic Manufacturing Co., 329 U.S. 394 (1947).

[55] American Auto Ass'n v. Spiegel, 205 F.2d 771 (2d Cir. 1953), cert. denied, 346 U.S. 887 (1953).

[56] Gray Tool Co. v. Humble Oil & Refining Co., 186 F.2d 365 (5th Cir. 1951), cert. denied, 341 U.S. 934 (1951).

[57] Perma Life Mufflers, Inc. v. International Parts Corp., 392 U.S. 134 (1968).

[58] Kelley v. Kosuga, 358 U.S. 516, 518 (1959).

[59] Cheff v. Schmackenberg, 384 U.S. 373 (1966).

[60] Utah Public Service Commission v. El Paso Natural Gas Company, 395 U.S. 464 (1969).

[61] Kiefer-Stewart Co. v. Joseph E. Seagram & Sons, Inc., 340 U.S. 211 (1951).

[62] Federal Trade Commission v. Universal-Rundle Corp., 387 U.S. 244 (1967).

faults under contract and tort laws on any such collateral grounds? Surely equal justice under the laws should apply in antitrust—as well as in other—proceedings.

6

THE OBSERVANCE OF
THE ANTITRUST LAWS

Comprehensive Analysis

The enforcement provisions of the antitrust laws are, of course, paralleled and supplemented by the compliance procedures of American industry. The mechanics for self-policing by industry are even more flexible than the enforcement alternatives that we have just reviewed. Indeed, the voluntary procedures for antitrust compliance are limited only by the resourcefulness of counsel and the resources of his company. As the lay reader will be particularly interested in comparing his own experiences with those of others in this phase of antitrust law, a brief review of these compliance techniques, currently in use, may be helpful.

Every responsible corporate program for compliance at least commences with some review of some areas in which the antitrust laws apply to the individual corporation. The breadth, depth, and accuracy of this survey will depend upon the extent to which the client wishes to ensure that counsel has a sound foundation of fact upon which to build, with his legal tools, an effective compliance structure. The recent series of jail sentences in antitrust proceedings emphasizes that a compliance program erected upon erroneous facts—due to the concealment of information from the practitioner—is no safeguard against confinement of executives in the penitentiary.

At the outset, counsel for the company usually surveys the impact of these laws upon the horizontal and vertical relationships of his client with competitors and customers. Thus, he customarily checks on all contacts of the corporation's personnel with those of competitors. Have there been discussions with those competitors concerning products to be offered, prices to be quoted, or customers to be sold? If so, have these discussions led to concerted restraints in pricing[1] or practices,[2] or were any effects the natural result of competition?[3] And what about the fairness of the client's competitive activities? Does the corporation engage in predatory pricing[4] or other exclusionary practices[5] which drive smaller competitors from the field? Again, counsel must review the selection of customers,[6] any discrimination between the customers chosen,[7] possible consignment arrangements,[8] and any tying or total requirement contracts.[9] From these issues he might broaden the inquiry to deal with such other activities as leasing,[10] licensing,[11] and purchasing.[12]

Once he has checked on these sensitive antitrust areas, he must proceed to evaluate these practices in the light of the relative position and power of his corporation in the industry. He should, of course, check the size of his client, for size has been called an earmark of monopoly power.[13] He may then proceed to determine the extent to which it is horizontally integrated in a series of geographic markets,[14] or is vertically integrated as both supplier and purchaser.[15] Its profit margins in the aggregate,[16] by divisions[17] and by products,[18] may be significant. From there he might look for prior acquisitions,[19] existing stockholdings in other companies,[20] and possible interlocking directorships.[21]

Finally, counsel will, if he is wise, check his findings against his company's files. In this connection the attorney must remember at all times that the most authoritative advice of compliance, dutifully followed, may avail little should a court find that the recommended lawful acts were undertaken pursuant to some written unlawful intent.[22]

---

[1] United States v. Container Corp. of America, 393 U.S. 333 (1969).
[2] Interstate Circuit, Inc. v. United States, 306 U.S. 208 (1939).
[3] Theatre Enterprises, Inc. v. Paramount Film Distributing Corp., 346 U.S. 537 (1954).
[4] Moore v. Mead's Fine Bread Company, 348 U.S. 115 (1954).
[5] International Salt Co., Inc. v. United States, 332 U.S. 392 (1947).
[6] Albrecht v. Herald Co., 390 U.S. 145 (1968).
[7] Federal Trade Commission v. Fred Meyer, Inc., 390 U.S. 341 (1968).
[8] Simpson v. Union Oil Co., 377 U.S. 13 (1964).
[9] Perma Life Mufflers, Inc. v. International Parts Corp., 392 U.S. 134 (1968); Fortner Enterprises, Inc. v. United States Steel Corp., 394 U.S. 495 (1969).
[10] United States v. United Shoe Machinery Corp., 110 F. Supp. 295 (D.Mass. 1953), aff'd, 347 U.S. 521 (1954).
[11] United States v. Glaxo Group Limited, 410 U.S. 52 (1973).
[12] United States v. Griffith, 334 U.S. 100 (1948).
[13] United States v. Paramount Pictures, Inc., 334 U.S. 131 (1948).
[14] Schine Chain Theatres, Inc. v. United States, 334 U.S. 110 (1948).
[15] United States v. Yellow Cab Co., 332 U.S. 218 (1947).
[16] United States v. General Electric Co., 82 F. Supp. 753 (D.N.J. 1949).
[17] United States v. New York Great Atlantic & Pacific Tea Co., 173 F.2d 79 (7th Cir. 1949).
[18] United States v. United Shoe Machinery Corp., 110 F. Supp. 295 (D.Mass. 1953), aff'd, 347 U.S. 521 (1954).
[19] Brown Shoe Co. v. United States, 370 U.S. 294 (1962).
[20] United States v. E. I. du Pont de Nemours & Company, 353 U.S. 586 (1957).
[21] United States v. Sears, Roebuck & Co., 111 F. Supp. 614 (S.D.N.Y. 1953).
[22] Hartford-Empire Co. v. United States, 323 U.S. 386 (1945); 324 U.S. 570 (1945).

This legal inventory of antitrust issues will necessarily proceed item by item. Needless to say, however, at the completion of the inventory the component corporate items must be carefully fitted together to form the composite corporate picture, because inoffensive individual parts may collectively disclose a very different antitrust totality. Counsel may find that each of ten contracts is lawful, whereas the ten collectively may show an unlawful pattern: "whatever we may think of them separately . . . [t]he plan may make the parts unlawful."[23]

Management Decisions

Every responsible corporate program for antitrust compliance must also involve some decision or decisions of management, with respect to the procedures to be established in the light of the foregoing legal audit. These procedures should ensure that the purpose and effect of the various relationships of the company, so reviewed, thereafter conform to the competitive objective of the antitrust laws, and safeguard against possible future abuse of the corporation's strength.

The compliance decisions of corporate management in a small company, after such an antitrust survey, are usually few in number. Any antitrust fires discovered in the course of counsel's inspection are put out. Then elementary precautions to avoid future conflagrations, as, for example, by eliminating debatable new competitive contacts, are customarily laid down. Warnings may also be issued with respect to mergers. Otherwise, the company generally tends to rely upon the availability of counsel to handle any further antitrust alarms on a "when and if" basis.

The compliance decisions of a large corporation, however, are usually more numerous and far-reaching. Counsel's antitrust surveys of such major companies ordinarily turn up perplexing problems, which may necessitate major changes in corporate policies. Thus the discovery of a pattern of autocratic leadership of an industry by a dominant company or group of companies may suggest a less dictatorial role in the future.[24] Again, any indication of a paternal patrolling of the resale prices,[25] territories,[26] and other dealings[27] of customers may require the emancipation of these economic serfs. Also, a pattern of collective action by members of a large corporate family against competitors may lead to instructions that each solvent corporate child

---

[23] Swift & Company v. United States, 196 U.S. 375, 396 (1905).
[24] American Tobacco Co. v. United States, 328 U.S. 781 (1946).
[25] United States v. Parke, Davis & Co., 362 U.S. 29 (1960); 365 U.S. 125 (1961).
[26] United States v. Topco Associates, Inc., 405 U.S. 596 (1972).
[27] Federal Trade Commission v. Brown Shoe Co., 384 U.S. 316 (1966).

that is able to do so should fight its own competitive battle, without undue future reliance upon the strength of a big corporate brother.[28] Alarming cracks of this nature in the antitrust fortifications of large integrated companies are often found to be concealed by the ivy of time.[29]

When a corporate defendant is subject to an antitrust judgment or order, its compliance decisions, in particular, must be made with great care. Counsel for such a defendant company frequently consults with the government agency responsible for the enforcement of this judgment or order, so as to ensure that its corporate decisions conform within reason to the governmental construction of this instrument. In such a case the Supreme Court has ruled that

> where the language of a consent decree in its normal meaning supports an interpretation; where that interpretation has been adhered to over many years by all parties, including those governmental officials who drew up and administered the decree from the start; and where the trial court concludes that this interpretation is in fact the one the parties intended, we will not reject it . . . .[30]

Supervised Decisions

A corporate program for antitrust compliance, to be effective, must further implement its policy decisions with executive directives calculated to make them operative. These directives, when well drafted, place upon designated officials the responsibility for executing specified compliance policies. Such directives should also be accompanied by provisions for the periodic reminder of those policies to old employees and the automatic furnishing of copies thereof to new employees. Armed with such executive directives, the corporation will be in a better position thereafter to demonstrate that any future irregular activities, such as the loose writings of sales personnel, which are contrary to these instructions, are not to be attributed to corporate executives but rather "are to be accounted for by the initiative of the sales agents and salesmen in their anxiety to make commissions . . . ."[31]

These executive directives, in some cases, should be followed up by a continuing educational campaign. Certain types of subordinates, and even some executives, are apt to treat such directives as

---

[28] Fortner Enterprises, Inc. v. United States Steel Corp., 394 U.S. 495 (1969).
[29] See, for example, United States v. Paramount Pictures, Inc., 334 U.S. 131 (1948).
[30] United States v. Atlantic Refining Co., 360 U.S. 19, 23–4 (1959).
[31] Patterson v. United States, 222 Fed. 599, 641 (6th Cir. 1915), *cert. denied,* 238 U.S. 635 (1915).

paper orders, issued solely for the record and in order to placate counsel. Branch and foreign offices are particularly inclined to interpret the law for themselves, without benefit of a legal education. Accordingly, some companies find it helpful to hold meetings of selected officers and employees from time to time, at which the meaning and application both of the antitrust laws generally, and of the corporate directives specifically, are carefully explained.

In particular, a successful compliance program seeks to drive home to corporate personnel that a businessman should not rely upon concealment as a substitute for compliance with these directives. If his own files do not incriminate him, the uninhibited memories of hostile ex-employees and the informative memoranda of methodical competitors will hasten to complete the record.[32] In the absence of written evidence, abnormal uniform price increases[33] or other inexplicable parallel conduct may read as clearly as photostats. The knowing acceptance of the benefits of restraints imposed by others similarly may suggest the existence of agreements, even if not reduced to writing.[34] One need not even formally agree with his competitors, to be held to be a co-conspirator: "It is elementary that an unlawful conspiracy may be and often is formed without simultaneous action or agreement on the part of the conspirators."[35]

Years ago the files of a trade association and of eight companies which were its members showed only the most innocuous of activities; but when the government got to the ninth, a confidential memorandum was found from the sales manager, which began: "By now you probably have received the lawyers' minutes of our last meeting, but let me tell you what really happened."

Above all, the advertising practices of large and small corporations alike must be policed in order to ensure that each new claim advanced to induce purchases by uninformed customers is reasonably substantiated,[36] at the time that the claim is advertised.[37] A compliance program is inadequate today if it merely avoids trade restraints. It must also measure its provisions against the evolving new yardsticks of courts and commission which seek to protect the purchasing public by application to industry practices of "the elusive, but congressionally mandated standard of fairness [which] considers pub-

[32] Richard Austin Smith, "The Incredible Electrical Conspiracy," *Fortune*, vol. 63 (April 1961), pp. 132–37 and (May 1961), pp. 161–164.
[33] American Tobacco Co. v. United States, 328 U.S. 781 (1946).
[34] Eugene Dietzgen Co. v. Federal Trade Commission, 142 F.2d 321 (7th Cir. 1944), *cert. denied*, 323 U.S. 730 (1944).
[35] Interstate Circuit, Inc. v. United States, 306 U.S. 208, 227 (1939).
[36] Pfizer, Inc., 81 FTC 23 (1972).
[37] Firestone Tire & Rubber Co. v. Federal Trade Commission, 481 F.2d 246 (6th Cir.), *cert. denied*, 414 U.S. 1112 (1973).

lic values beyond those enshrined in the letter or encompassed in the spirit of the antitrust laws."[38]

Recorded Decisions

The corporate management which has formulated its antitrust decisions and has in good faith taken steps to ensure their implementation also considers how it can and should record this program. All too frequently a hostile investigator discovers half-truths in written form and the defendant—to present the complete verity—must hastily improvise its proofs through witnesses who are suspect because they are interested: "Where such testimony is in conflict with contemporaneous documents we can give it little weight . . . ."[39]

The most elementary procedure for recording a compliance program is to see to it that the corporation makes its record of compliance before, rather than after, it is investigated. The contemporaneous evidence of the events and underlying considerations leading up to and immediately following a significant corporate decision should be put in writing and so be preserved. Thus, when a company acquires another corporation, it is essential that written evidence of the reasons for the acquisition, and of the absence of any attendant injury to competition, be marshaled. Also, if following a major decision of a corporation some competitor drops out of the commercial struggle, without being pushed, it is a sound precaution to collect promptly all readily accessible written evidence which establishes the true reasons for that failure.

A supplemental form of recording a compliance program relates to the proper handling of the occasional colorful prose of irresponsible employees. Inevitably, in the operations of any large corporation, some imaginative correspondent will flatly contradict, and thereby tend to undermine, the most conservative program of antitrust compliance, thereby inviting a judicial ruling that such "writings made contemporaneously with events as they were occurring . . . give ample evidence of 'an ever present manifestation of conscious wrongdoing.' "[40]

In such an event, it is advisable not to destroy these picturesque writings.[41] The mere destruction of such writings, unless explained,

---

[38] Federal Trade Commission v. Sperry & Hutchinson Co., 405 U.S. 233, 244 (1972).
[39] United States v. United States Gypsum Co., 333 U.S. 364, 396 (1948).
[40] United States v. Hartford-Empire Co., 46 F. Supp. 541, 610 (N.D.Ohio 1942), *rev'd on other grounds,* 323 U.S. 386 and 324 U.S. 570 (1945).
[41] Stoumen v. Commissioner of Internal Revenue, 208 F.2d 903 (3d Cir. 1953). See also the Federal Trade Commission Act sec. 10, 38 Stat. 723 (1914), *as amended,* 15 U.S.C. sec. 50 (1970).

may give rise to an inference of wrongful conduct.[42] Instead, it is best to answer the colorful document in writing, point by point, and to place both the original and the answer in the company's files. If the matter is sufficiently serious, the corporation might also follow through by doing some affirmative corporate act directly disproving the unlawful assertions of the unauthorized writer.

The importance of accurate records in a program of antitrust compliance cannot be stressed too strongly. In most of the transactions in which a corporate executive wishes to engage, his intent usually conforms to the intent of the antitrust laws. The mechanics for implementing this intent, however, are not always planned in a manner to make manifest this lawful purpose. If the executive will only consult his counsel sufficiently in advance of a proposed major transaction, the step-by-step negotiation and formalization of the original lawful purpose can be so guided and recorded that his actions similarly will be in accord with the requirements of these laws, and the supporting evidence of his antitrust compliance will be available if needed later on. A stitch of antitrust advice in time may well save the subsequent payment of an antitrust fine.

---

[42] A. C. Becken Co. v. Gemex Corporation, 314 F.2d 839 (7th Cir. 1963), *cert. denied,* 375 U.S. 816 (1963).

7

THE EFFECTS OF
THE ANTITRUST LAWS

Individual Hardships

The lay reader has now painfully climbed the sides of our antitrust laws noting, in passing, their words, interpretations, and implementations. His inspection necessarily has been limited to surface impressions of this legislation, but his examination nevertheless has enabled him to sense their general contours. He might now pause at the summit and observe the part which these laws play in the surrounding terrain of the overall economy.

Understandably, his immediate reaction may be that the impact of these laws upon the individual businessman at best has been unpredictable and at worst has been unpleasant—confirming his original impression of this legislation as outlined in the introductory remarks of this monograph. The laws have been unpredictable because the corporate executive has been able to rely neither upon precision in the congressional legislation nor upon precedent in their judicial construction. Their composite command that he observe loosely formulated standards, based upon economic, political, and ethical theories, has at times bewildered even his counsel. These laws, moreover, have been unpleasant on those occasions when civil and criminal penalties have been imposed upon him for departing from the current commands of this confusing legislation. The industrialist can justifiably complain of cruel and unusual punishment when he suffers personal indignity and property losses for failing to conform his conduct to the uncertain statutory standards of effective competition, when even the courts concede, "The precise ingredients of 'effective competition' cannot be said to have been a static concept . . . . Their applications, as well as their implications, have varied with changes in judicial thought with respect to economic and legal philosophies."[1]

The objective reader will further observe that, in the treatment of these laws by the three branches of our government, there has been no sustained drive to soften this adverse impact upon the harassed businessman. The enforcement agencies, for example, have normally preferred to wield the club in lieu of offering the carrot to achieve antitrust enforcement. Seldom have these agencies announced their proposed new interpretations in advance and offered an antitrust moratorium, during which industry would be permitted voluntarily to elect whether or not to acquiesce therein. Instead, both the Department of Justice and the Federal Trade Commission have been accustomed to thrust even their new views upon the businessman in the course of extensive investigation and expensive litigation, in which they have sought criminal sanctions,[2] divestiture,[3] and/or sweeping orders to cease and desist.[4] Recently the commission has had serious second thoughts with respect to the injustice of proceeding against businessmen guilty only of good faith reliance upon past interpretations of applicable trade regulation laws, and has established imaginative procedures seeking to give advance notice of new commission views through opinions, guides, and rules. The department, however, in contrast, currently seems willing to dispense only with criminal proceedings when it seeks to extend the frontiers of our antitrust laws.

Similarly the courts, on their part, have not been content to discharge prospectively their quasi-legislative duties. Rather, when they have adopted clarifying new interpretations proposed by public and private plaintiffs, they have all too frequently applied retroactively their new trade regulations. *Ex post facto* decisions have penalized defendants for engaging in judicially sanctioned industry practices of long standing as, for example, in leasing,[5] in licensing,[6] and in selling through agents.[7] The courts have performed well their delegated functions of evolving, case by case, the meaning and application of congressional principles, but they have rarely assumed any

---

[1] United States v. Aluminum Company of America, 91 F. Supp. 333, 340 (S.D.N.Y. 1950). Cf. Tampa Electric Co. v. Nashville Coal Co., 365 U.S. 320 (1961).
[2] United States v. South-Eastern Underwriters Association, 322 U.S. 533 (1944).
[3] United States v. E. I. du Pont de Nemours & Company, 353 U.S. 586 (1957).
[4] Federal Trade Commission v. National Lead Co., 352 U.S. 419 (1957).
[5] United States v. United Shoe Machinery Corp., 110 F. Supp. 295 (D. Mass. 1953), aff'd, 347 U.S. 521 (1954); Hanover Shoe, Inc. v. United Shoe Machinery Corp., 391 U.S. 481 (1968); United States v. United Shoe Machinery Corp., 391 U.S. 244 (1968).
[6] United States v. Line Material Co., 333 U.S. 287 (1948); Zenith Radio Corporation v. Hazeltine Research, Inc., 395 U.S. 100 (1969).
[7] Simpson v. Union Oil Co., 377 U.S. 13 (1964); Simpson v. Union Oil Co. of Calif., 396 U.S. 13 (1969).

responsibility for mitigating the backward sweep of their rulings upon the industrial principals. The destruction of patent property in the course of evolving new judicial antitrust laws is illustrative of this notable absence of judicial due process.[8]

Congress, moreover, has seldom encouraged the other branches of the government to minimize unnecessary hardships upon business in the application of the antitrust laws. Its committees seem indifferent to the problems inherent in complying with generally phrased legislation and to the attendant justice of softening the retroactive impact of new judicial rulings upon the industrial community. No distinctions have as yet been made in statutory provisions for fines, jail, and treble damages between the intentional and the unintentional wrongdoer. The interest on Capitol Hill would appear rather to lie in the encouragement of more numerous enforcement proceedings and in more painful antitrust penalties.

The disinterested observer might well applaud the suggestion made in connection with one of the recent retroactive rulings of the Supreme Court: "Surely there is merit to the notion of shaping the punishment to fit the crime, even beyond the precincts of the mikado's palace."[9]

Free Economy

Hopefully, however, the more considered impression of the lay observer will be that the general impact of the antitrust laws upon our society, as distinguished from its specific effect upon individual businessmen, has been most salutary.

The primary justification for our antitrust laws has been their contribution to the preservation in this nation, as intended by Congress, of a free economy. The monopolies and trusts of the late nineteenth century have been broken up. The regulators of the early twentieth century who governed trade through NRA codes,[10] patent licenses,[11] and trade associations[12] have been outlawed. Horizontal conspiracies between competitors and vertical domination of distributors have been discouraged. As a result, "The basic industries, with few exceptions, do not approach in America a cartelized form."[13]

---

[8] For example, see United States v. Glaxo Group Limited, 410 U.S. 52 (1973).

[9] United States v. E. I. du Pont de Nemours & Company, 366 U.S. 316, 371 (1961) (Frankfurter, J., dissenting opinion).

[10] A. L. A. Schechter Poultry Corp. v. United States, 295 US. 495 (1935).

[11] Hartford-Empire Co. v. United States, 324 U.S. 570 (1945).

[12] Sugar Institute, Inc. v. United States, 297 U.S. 553 (1936).

[13] United States v. Columbia Steel Co., 334 U.S. 495, 526 (1948).

Our economy has been free to enjoy the fruits of large[14] as well as of small companies, integrated[15] as well as single-function organizations. The number of competitors in any one industry has been deemed to be irrelevant so long as they compete.[16] Cooperative endeavors in the form of joint ventures[17] and trade associations[18] have been encouraged, although certain qualifications for participation and the permissible scope of their activities have been established.[19] Freedom of entry into the market, above all, has been jealously guarded.[20]

The attendant material progress of our society, derived in part at least from our antitrust laws, has, of course, been self-evident. True, the richness of our natural resources, the explosive blending of the racial skills of our polyglot people, and the continental sweep of our industrial markets largely have made possible this material progress. Nevertheless, our antitrust laws have contributed to the creation and nurture of a challenging environment which has encouraged individual intiative to exploit these God- and man-made opportunities in a market relatively free of private and public restraint.

The intangible value of economic freedom, moreover, has also been very real. The businessman has been forced to suffer the slings and arrows of disturbing litigation launched under uncertain statutes, but he has thereby avoided the far graver ills of private or public monopoly. The antitrust laws have provided him with a substantial shelter both from the antisocial reactionary of the right and the revolutionary socialist on the left. The price of this liberty may be eternal vigilance on his part to detect disturbing new developments as they appear on the uncertain antitrust horizon, but at least this liberty leaves him with the competitive opportunities of a free economy to console him for paying this price.

Democratic Economy

A secondary, but still pronounced, contribution of our antitrust laws has been their assistance to other influential forces in encouraging the development of a democratic economy. On the one hand, companies of large size have been bluntly informed that size is an earmark of monopoly power which may not be abused.[21] The growth of large

---

[14] United States v. United States Steel Corporation, 251 U.S. 417 (1920).
[15] United States v. Aluminum Company of America, 91 F. Supp. 333 (S.D.N.Y. 1950).
[16] United States v. National Lead Co., 332 U.S. 319 (1947).
[17] United States v. Morgan, 118 F. Supp. 621 (S.D.N.Y. 1953).
[18] Maple Flooring Manufacturers Ass'n v. United States, 268 U.S. 563 (1925).
[19] United States v. Penn-Olin Chem. Co., 378 U.S. 158 (1964); Fashion Originators' Guild of America, Inc. v. Federal Trade Commission, 312 U.S. 457 (1941).
[20] International Salt Co., Inc. v. United States, 332 U.S. 392 (1947).
[21] United States v. Paramount Pictures, Inc., 334 U.S. 131 (1948).

aggregations of capital through using the leverage of their integrated strength in buying[22] and distributing,[23] and through taking over substantial competitors and customers,[24] has been restricted. Moreover, new limitations upon growth through acquisitions are being imposed.[25] On the other hand, the competitive disadvantage of the small retailer has been alleviated by the prohibition of unjustified differentials in prices[26] and promotions.[27] Under the antitrust laws, large and small have been viewed to be equal, with possibly an inclination to prefer the small as a little more equal. No businessman is denied protection "merely because the victim is just one merchant whose business is so small that his destruction makes little difference to the economy."[28]

Our economy is, of course, reflecting the worldwide trend to units of large size. Just as the city was merged into the state, and the state into the nation, so the individual partnership is being replaced by the regional company and the regional company by the national corporation. Our society, however, has found it possible to reconcile local self-government with national government. Similarly, we are finding ways and means of utilizing the personal, specialized skills of the small merchant to supplement the impersonal, mass-produced products and services of the large enterprise.

The small businessman may not safely be shielded from competition. He must justify his existence by proving that, in highly individualized phases of industry, he is able to provide goods and services tailored to the special needs of the public in a manner which cannot be offered profitably by the corporate giant. Anyone who fails so to justify his role in industry by making a significant contribution to our economy should bow out without seeking to burden the consumer with a subsidy to finance his industrial featherbedding. Today, as of old, however, the business David who selects carefully his battleground should and will continue to triumph.

Ethical Economy

The least publicized contribution of the antitrust laws has been their role in lending support to other influences in encouraging the growth of an ethical economy, yet this moral development is also very real. A

---

[22] Federal Trade Commission v. Consolidated Foods Corp., 380 U.S. 592 (1965).
[23] United States v. National Dairy Prods. Corp., 372 U.S. 29 (1963).
[24] Brown Shoe Co. v. United States, 370 U.S. 294 (1962).
[25] United States v. Falstaff Brewing Corporation, 410 U.S. 526 (1973); Federal Trade Commission v. Procter & Gamble Co., 386 U.S. 568 (1967).
[26] Perkins v. Standard Oil Company of California, 393 U.S. 1013 (1969).
[27] Federal Trade Commission v. Fred Meyer, Inc., 390 U.S. 341 (1968).
[28] Klor's, Inc. v. Broadway-Hale Stores, Inc., 359 U.S. 207, 213 (1959).

review of early antitrust decisions emphasizes how far we have come from the days of the fighting ships,[29] concealed subsidiaries,[30] bribery,[31] sabotage,[32] and predatory cutting off of essential sources of supply.[33] In part by reason of these laws, today we seldom run into the lack of business ethics of the uninhibited era of our forefathers which permitted deliberate efforts to control trade "by methods devised in order to monopolize the trade by driving competitors out of business, which were ruthlessly carried out . . . ."[34]

The Federal Trade Commission, in particular, has taken giant strides to cleanse the byways and airways of our economy. Armed with adequate powers to proceed against unfair and deceptive acts and practices, without the necessity to prove any specific injury to competition, the commission in recent years has moved with increasing vigor against individual minor, but collectively substantial, devices to mislead and mistreat the overly trusting consumer. Its drive to promote truth in advertising, moreover, is being increasingly effective despite omnipotent critics who assert that it simultaneously is both proceeding much too slowly and also far too fast in this evolving area of the law.[35]

Admittedly much remains to be done. Indeed, when we look ahead we may become discouraged by the distance yet to be covered. If we look back, however, we are entitled to be encouraged by noting how far we have come. The dogma of Karl Marx that the competition of capitalism will necessarily lead to jungle warfare, in which competitor will eat competitor until only monopoly remains, has been refuted by our antitrust laws. The ethical merchant has not only survived but has been successful. We commendably take pride in the economic and political progress of our economy, but we may also be proud of the slow but increasing growth of our industrial conscience.

In the last analysis, therefore, the objective of the antitrust laws has not been the "radical" desire to destroy, but rather the "reactionary" endeavor to defend, private enterprise, through harnessing it to produce a free, democratic, ethical economy. Not without reason, accordingly, do the principles underlying these laws today enjoy the support of such diverse groups as the Democratic and Republican

---

[29] Thomsen v. Cayser, 243 U.S. 66 (1917).
[30] United States v. American Can Co., 230 Fed. 859 (D.Md. 1916).
[31] American Steel Co. v. American Steel & Wire Co., 244 Fed. 300 (D.Mass. 1916).
[32] Patterson v. United States, 222 Fed. 599 (6th Cir. 1915), *cert. denied*, 238 U.S. 635 (1915).
[33] United States v. Reading Company, 226 U.S. 324 (1912).
[34] United States v. American Tobacco Company, 221 U.S. 106, 181 (1911).
[35] Federal Trade Commission v. Sperry & Hutchinson Co., 405 U.S. 233 (1972); see generally, "Misrepresentation," "False Advertising," and "Unfair Practices," 2 CCH Trade Reg. Rep. para. 7521 et seq.

parties, the AFL-CIO, the National Association of Manufacturers, and the United States Chamber of Commerce.

Indeed, not the least of the contributions of these laws may be that by reason thereof businessmen are unable safely to "rest upon their oars"—self-satisfied with past successes—but instead are ever challenged by innovative competitors to continue their efforts to reduce costs, improve quality, and develop new products and services. In this manner, our industrialists are forced constantly to be creative in improving our American way of life. In contrast, past civilizations seem to have broken down principally due "to the spiritual demoralization to which we human beings seem to be prone on the morrow of great achievements—a demoralization to which we are not bound to succumb, and for which we ourselves therefore bear the responsibility. Success seems to make us lazy or self-satisfied or conceited."[36]

---

[36] Arnold Toynbee, *A Study of History* (New York: McGraw-Hill, 1972), p. 141.

8

THE MODEST CONCLUSION

These pages have sought to explain that the congressional objective of our antitrust laws has been to prohibit private restraints which may operate to deny to our nation a competitive economy; that the judicial application of these laws has been to promote this objective in order to achieve, through a competitive economy, the three-fold blessings of material prosperity, political democracy, and an ethical society; and that their resulting impact by operation of involuntary proceedings and voluntary procedures—while harsh upon individual businessmen—has been salutary to our society. Therefore, to the reader's possible dismay, the author will now in conclusion propose no statutory changes to clarify these laws, no judicial standards to give precision to their interpretations, nor any other comparable changes of a *substantive* nature.

There is of course no lack of planned programs for antitrust reformation, earnestly advanced by antitrust protestants. These thoughtful suggestions seek to have us choose among the economic, political, and ethical reasons for a competitive economy and, by concentrating upon one motivation, to clarify and simplify the interpretation and application of the laws fostering such an economy. Thus, economists have proposed the use of qualitative standards of industrial efficiency, technological progress, variable profits, and freedom of entry to ensure a productive society. Again, political scientists have offered quantitative yardsticks, which count the number and limit the relative size of competitors in an industry, to guarantee a democratic society. And moral idealists have offered germicidal brooms of differing shapes and sizes with which to sweep clean the commercial stables.

We are not presently content in this country, however, to limit our laws to the achievement of any one of these proposed reforms. Congress and courts correctly recognize that we seek a competitive economy in order simultaneously to promote our material, our political, and our moral welfare, and that we will not settle for a single antitrust standard of interpretation which exalts one at the expense of the other of these earnestly sought benefits. We therefore insist that these statutes continue to incorporate our multiple desires for an ideal society in which industrial prosperity, economic power, and commercial purity are to be distributed—through competition—to all, and to instruct our courts and agencies to secure to us, as best they may, these conflicting, confusing, but cherished dreams. True, we may never reach the fabled walls of our antitrust Carcassonne, but we will take only a road which leads in its direction.

We are probably wiser by reason of our legal traditions in requiring Congress and courts to cling to these illusive ideals, moreover, than are the experts in advancing their sensible solutions. The checks and balances of our Constitution have worked in this country because they have permitted us to resolve disputes between the three divisions of our government through the art of practical compromise. Similarly the checks and balances of the economic, political, and ethical motivation of our antitrust laws may have worked, at least in this country, because they have enabled us to resolve debates with respect to the three-fold purposes of this legislation through the process of judicial compromise.

The author's reluctance to champion any change of a substantive nature in our antitrust laws does not indicate, however, that he considers whatever is to be right. On the contrary, he views the occasional harsh impact of these laws—arising from the uncertain generalities of their provisions—to be an unnecessary by-product of this otherwise commendable legislation. Accordingly, he does at least make two modest *procedural* proposals to soften any unconscionable impact of these laws upon individual businessmen.

The initial suggestion is that an industry, wishing to clarify and thereby avoid any unanticipated application of the antitrust laws to its products and services, might propose specific guides or rules to the government and obtain authoritative rulings thereon. Such guides or rules—after review and refinement by Washington—could be controlling unless and until such official approval is withdrawn. Thereafter, the private proponents might cooperate with the public prosecutors to ensure uniform, industrywide observance of the resulting regulations. For those interested, there are procedures presently available in the Federal Trade Commission to implement this proposal.[1]

---

[1] For further details, see Van Cise, "Regulation—By Business or Government," *Harvard Business Review,* vol. 44 (1966), p. 53.

The further suggestion is that the three branches of our government might in their turn consider whether new interpretations of the antitrust laws need always be applied retroactively. Our antitrust laws, in effect, reward the industrial giant of our economy for its services to society by chaining it to what usually are uncertain rules which permit doubts of the legal unknown to attack its vital operations. These industry fears for the future are then magnified manyfold by the unhappy knowledge that as new interpretations of these laws evolve, onerous litigation and oppressive penalties may be thrust even upon the businessman who seeks conscientiously to conform to these laws. It is submitted that clarification in this manner need not thus be synonymous with callousness to persons and confiscation of property. We should rather earnestly explore legislative, administrative, and judicial procedures through which to avoid where possible, and to soften in any event, the retroactive impact of antitrust change so frequently experienced in the application of these laws. As the Federal Trade Commission is commencing to recognize, the businessman should be held strictly accountable for his travels in the settled areas of antitrust prohibitions, but ways and means should be found of permitting him to adjust, without *ex post facto* punishment, to newly developed or rezoned regions of these regulations. If baseball may rely upon past judicial rulings,[2] may not others who earn their livelihood from competition?

To summarize, therefore, today we enjoy the blessings of life, liberty, and the right to choose the pursuit which best promises us happiness. The antitrust burdens currently imposed upon business may well have freed us from the necessity to surrender our persons and our property to the state. We should seek, where possible, to clarify and minimize the retroactive impact of these business burdens, in the manner just suggested, but we should otherwise continue our efforts through these laws to maximize the attendant social blessings. Our American dream, in which the antitrust laws play an imperfect role, may be illusory; but at least it is better thus to dream, in a free society, than to cower behind cement walls in a communistic state.

---

[2] Flood v. Kuhn, 407 U.S. 258 (1972).

APPENDIX A
Provisions of Statutes

Sherman Antitrust Act Sections 1-3 (15 U.S.C.A. Sections 1-3)

Section 1. Every contract, combination in the form of trust or otherwise, or conspiracy, in restraint of trade or commerce among the several States, or with foreign nations, is declared to be illegal . . . . Every person who shall make any contract or engage in any combination or conspiracy declared by sections 1 to 7 of this title to be illegal shall be deemed guilty of a felony, and, on conviction thereof, shall be punished by fine not exceeding one million dollars if a corporation or, if any other person, one hundred thousand dollars or by imprisonment not exceeding three years, or by both said punishments, in the discretion of the court. [2 July 1890, chap. 647, sec. 1, 26 Stat. 209, *as amended,* 15 U.S.C.A. sec. 1 (Supp. I 1975)]

Section 2. Every person who shall monopolize, or attempt to monopolize, or combine or conspire with any other person or persons, to monopolize any part of the trade or commerce among the several States, or with foreign nations, shall be deemed guilty of a felony, and, on conviction thereof, shall be punished by fine not exceeding one million dollars if a corporation or, if any other person, one hundred thousand dollars or by imprisonment not exceeding three years, or by both said punishments, in the discretion of the court. [2 July 1890, chap. 647, sec. 2, 26 Stat. 209, *as amended,* 15 U.S.C.A. sec. 2 (Supp. I 1975)]

Section 3. Every contract, combination in form of trust or otherwise, or conspiracy, in restraint of trade or commerce in any Territory of the

Note: The statutory provisions quoted herein are, of course, supplemented by additional procedural and substantive legislation. If interested in these further details, the reader might consult the Commerce Clearing House, Inc., *Trade Regulation Reporter.* See, in particular, volume 4 of this service.

United States or of the District of Columbia, or in restraint of trade or commerce between any such Territory and another, or between any such Territory or Territories and any State or States or the District of Columbia, or with foreign nations, or between the District of Columbia and any State or States or foreign nations, is declared illegal. Every person who shall make any such contract or engage in any such combination or conspiracy, shall be deemed guilty of a felony, and, on conviction thereof, shall be punished by fine not exceeding one million dollars if a corporation or, if any other person, one hundred thousand dollars or by imprisonment not exceeding three years, or by both said punishments, in the discretion of the court. [2 July 1890, chap. 647, sec. 3, 26 Stat. 209, *as amended*, 15 U.S.C.A. sec. 3 (Supp. I 1975)]

Clayton Antitrust Act Sections 2, 3, and 7 (15 U.S.C. Sections 13, 14, and 18)

Section 2. [For provisions of section 2, see the amendatory Robinson-Patman Act Section 1.]

Section 3. That it shall be unlawful for any person engaged in commerce, in the course of such commerce, to lease or make a sale or contract for sale of goods, wares, merchandise, machinery, supplies or other commodities, whether patented or unpatented, for use, consumption or resale within the United States or any Territory thereof or the District of Columbia or any insular possession or other place under the jurisdiction of the United States, or fix a price charged therefor, or discount from, or rebate upon, such price, on the condition, agreement or understanding that the lessee or purchaser thereof shall not use or deal in the goods, wares, merchandise, machinery, supplies or other commodities of a competitor or competitors of the lessor or seller where the effect of such lease, sale, or contract for sale or such condition, agreement or understanding may be to substantially lessen competition or tend to create a monopoly in any line of commerce. [15 October 1914, chap. 323, sec. 3, 38 Stat. 731, *as amended*, 15 U.S.C. sec. 14]

Section 7. That no corporation engaged in commerce shall acquire, directly or indirectly, the whole or any part of the stock or other share capital and no corporation subject to the jurisdiction of the Federal Trade Commission shall acquire the whole or any part of the assets of another corporation engaged also in commerce, where in any line of commerce in any section of the country, the effect of such acquisition may be substantially to lessen competition, or to tend to create a monopoly. [15 October 1914, chap. 323, sec. 7, 38 Stat. 731, *as amended*, 15 U.S.C. sec. 18]

No corporation shall acquire, directly or indirectly, the whole or any part of the stock or other share capital and no corporation subject to the jurisdiction of the Federal Trade Commission shall acquire the whole or any part of the assets of one or more corporations engaged in commerce, where in any line of commerce in any section of the country, the effect of such acquisition, of such stocks or assets, or of the use of such stock by the voting or granting of proxies or otherwise, may be substantially to lessen competition, or to tend to create a monopoly. [15 October 1914, chap. 323, sec. 7, 38 Stat. 731, *as amended*, 15 U.S.C. sec. 18]

This section shall not apply to corporations purchasing such stock solely for investment and not using the same by voting or otherwise to bring about, or in attempting to bring about, the substantial lessening of competition. Nor shall anything contained in this section prevent a corporation engaged in commerce from causing the formation of subsidiary corporations for the actual carrying on of their immediate lawful business, or the natural and legitimate branches or extensions thereof, or from owning and holding all or a part of the stock of such subsidiary corporations, when the effect of such formation is not to substantially lessen competition. [15 October 1914, chap. 323, sec. 7, 38 Stat. 731, *as amended*, 15 U.S.C. sec. 18]

Nor shall anything herein contained be construed to prohibit any common carrier subject to the laws to regulate commerce from aiding in the construction of branches or short lines so located as to become feeders to the main line of the company so aiding in such construction or from acquiring or owning all or any part of the stock of such branch lines, nor to prevent any such common carrier from acquiring and owning all or any part of the stock of a branch or short line constructed by an independent company where there is no substantial competition between the company owning the branch line so constructed and the company owning the main line acquiring the property or an interest therein, nor to prevent such common carrier from extending any of its lines through the medium of the acquisition of stock or otherwise of any other common carrier where there is no substantial competition between the company extending its lines and the company whose stock, property, or an interest therein is so acquired. [15 October 1914, chap. 323, sec. 7, 38 Stat. 731, *as amended*, 15 U.S.C. sec. 18]

Nothing contained in this section shall be held to affect or impair any right heretofore legally acquired: *Provided*, That nothing in this section shall be held or construed to authorize or make lawful anything heretofore prohibited or made illegal by the antitrust laws, nor to exempt any person from the penal provisions thereof or the civil remedies therein provided. [15 October 1914, chap. 323, sec. 7, 38 Stat. 731, *as amended*, 15 U.S.C. sec. 18]

Nothing contained in this section shall apply to transactions duly consummated pursuant to authority given by the Civil Aeronautics Board, Federal Communications Commission, Federal Power Commission, Interstate Commerce Commission, the Securities and Exchange Commission in the exercise of its jurisdiction under section 10 of the Public Utility Holding Company Act of 1935, the United States Maritime Commission or the Secretary of Agriculture under any statutory provision vesting such power in such Commission, Secretary, or Board. [15 October 1914, chap. 323, sec. 7, 38 Stat. 731, *as amended*, 15 U.S.C. sec. 18]

Robinson-Patman Act Sections 1 and 3 (15 U.S.C. Sections 13 and 13a)

Section 1 (a) [Clayton Act Section 2]. That it shall be unlawful for any person engaged in commerce, in the course of such commerce, either directly or indirectly, to discriminate in price between different purchasers of commodities of like grade and quality, where either or any of the purchases involved in such discrimination are in commerce, where such commodities are sold for use, consumption, or resale within the United States or any Territory thereof or the District of Columbia or any insular possession or other place under the jurisdiction of the United States, and where the effect of such discrimination may be substantially to lessen competition or tend to create a monopoly in any line of commerce, or to injure, destroy, or prevent competition with any person who either grants or knowingly receives the benefit of such discrimination, or with customers of either of them: *Provided*, That nothing herein contained shall prevent differentials which make only due allowance for differences in the cost of manufacture, sale, or delivery resulting from the differing methods or quantities in which such commodities are to such purchasers sold or delivered: *Provided, however*, That the Federal Trade Commission may, after due investigation and hearing to all interested parties, fix and establish quantity limits, and revise the same as it finds necessary, as to particular commodities or classes of commodities, where it finds that available purchasers in greater quantities are so few as to render differentials on account thereof unjustly discriminatory or promotive of monopoly in any line of commerce; and the foregoing shall then not be construed to permit differentials based on differences in quantities greater than those so fixed and established: *And provided further*, That nothing herein contained shall prevent persons engaged in selling goods, wares, or merchandise in commerce from selecting their own customers in bona fide transactions and not in restraint of trade: *And provided further*, That nothing herein contained shall prevent price changes from time to time where in response to changing conditions affecting the market for or the marketability of the goods concerned, such as but not limited to actual or imminent deterioration of perishable goods, obsolescence of seasonal goods, distress sales under court process, or sales in good faith in discontinuance of business in the goods concerned. [19 June 1936, chap. 592, sec. 1, 49 Stat. 1526, *as amended*, 15 U.S.C. sec. 13]

(b) Upon proof being made, at any hearing on a complaint under this section, that there has been discrimination in price or services or facilities furnished, the burden of rebutting the prima-facie case thus made by showing justification shall be upon the person charged with a violation of this section, and unless justification shall be affirmatively shown, the Commission is authorized to issue an order terminating the discrimination: *Provided, however*, That nothing herein contained shall prevent a seller rebutting the prima-facie case thus made by showing that his lower price or the furnishing of services or facilities to any purchaser or purchasers was made in good faith to meet an equally low price of a competitor, or the services or facilities furnished by a competitor. [19 June 1936, chap. 592, sec. 1, 49 Stat. 1526, *as amended*, 15 U.S.C. sec. 13]

(c) That it shall be unlawful for any person engaged in commerce, in the course of such commerce, to pay or grant, or to receive or accept, anything of value as a commission, brokerage, or other compensation, or any allowance or discount in lieu thereof, except for services rendered in connection with the sale or purchase of goods, wares, or merchandise, either to the other party to such transaction or to an agent, representative, or other intermediary therein where such intermediary is acting in fact for or in behalf, or is subject to the direct or indirect control of any party to such transaction other than the person by whom such compensation is so granted or paid. [19 June 1936, chap. 592, sec. 1, 49 Stat. 1526, *as amended*, 15 U.S.C. sec. 13]

(d) That it shall be unlawful for any person engaged in commerce to pay or contract for the payment of anything of value to or for the benefit of a customer of such person in the course of such commerce as compensation or in consideration for any services or facilities furnished by or through such customer in connection with the processing, handling, sale, or offering for sale of any products or commodities manufactured, sold, or offered for sale by such person, unless such payment or consideration is available on proportionally equal terms to all other customers competing in the distribution of such products or commodities. [19 June 1936, chap. 592, sec. 1, 49 Stat. 1526, *as amended*, 15 U.S.C. sec. 13]

(e) That it shall be unlawful for any person to discriminate in favor of one purchaser against another purchaser or purchasers of a commodity bought for resale, with or without processing, by contracting to furnish or furnishing, or by contributing to the furnishing of, any services or facilities connected with the processing, handling, sale, or offering for sale of such commodity so purchased, upon terms not accorded to all purchasers on proportionally equal terms. [19 June 1936, chap. 592, sec. 1, 49 Stat. 1526, *as amended*, 15 U.S.C. sec. 13]

(f) That it shall be unlawful for any person engaged in commerce, in the course of such commerce, knowingly to induce or receive a discrimination in price which is prohibited by this section. [19 June 1936, chap. 592, sec. 1, 49 Stat. 1526, *as amended*, 15 U.S.C. sec. 13]

Section 3. It shall be unlawful for any person engaged in commerce, in the course of such commerce, to be a party to, or assist in, any transaction of sale, or contract to sell, which discriminates to his knowledge against competitors of the purchaser, in that, any discount, rebate, allowance, or advertising service charge is granted to the purchaser over and above any discount, rebate, allowance, or advertising service charge available at the time of such transaction to said competitors in respect of a sale of goods of like grade, quality, and quantity; to sell, or contract to sell, goods in any part of the United States at prices lower than those exacted by said person elsewhere in the United States for the purpose of destroying competition, or eliminating a competitor in such part of the United States; or, to sell, or contract to sell, goods at unreasonably low prices for the purpose of destroying competition or eliminating a competitor.

Any person violating any of the provisions of this section shall, upon conviction thereof, be fined not more than $5,000 or imprisoned not more than one year, or both. [19 June 1936, chap. 592, sec. 3, 49 Stat. 1528, *as amended*, 15 U.S.C. sec. 13a]

Federal Trade Commission Act Section 5 (a) (1) (15 U.S.C.A. Section 45)

Section 5(a)(1). Unfair methods of competition in or affecting commerce, and unfair or deceptive acts or practices in or affecting commerce, are declared unlawful. [26 September 1914, chap. 311, sec. 5, 38 Stat. 719, *as amended*, 15 U.S.C.A. sec. 45 (Supp. I 1975)]

APPENDIX B
Table of Authorities

Cases

Statutes

6603